About the Author

Former English Program Consultant at Dhofar University in Oman city of Salala, and freshman English instructor at The American University of Beirut, Lebanon. Author of Palestinian Villages Destroyed in the 1948 Fighting: *Alzeeb village as I Knew it* (Arabic).

O My Lord! Prayer in the Holy
Book of Muslims

Ahmad Awdeh

O My Lord! Prayer in the Holy Book of Muslims

Olympia Publishers
London

www.olympiapublishers.com
OLYMPIA PAPERBACK EDITION

A CIP catalogue record for this title is
available from the British Library.

ISBN: 978-1-80439-423-6

This is a book of prayers that are raised to God by angels, prophets,
believers and unbelievers. It presents these prayers contextualized,
some by a narrative and the others by a description of the situation in
which the prayer was raised. The prayers themselves are copied from
The Holy Book of Muslims, and their contexts are from information in
the neighboring verses and commentators' footnotes.

First Published in 2023

Olympia Publishers
Tallis House
2 Tallis Street
London
EC4Y 0AB

Printed in Great Britain

Acknowledgements

I wish to thank the translators and commentators of The Holy Qur'an: English Translation of the Meanings and Commentary at King Fahd Holy Qur'an Printing Complex at the city of Al Madinah, KSA, from which I took the prayer verses, and for their Commentary information from which I wrote the circumstances in which the prayers were raised. Finally, I wish to thank Mariam Saadedine for checking through the manuscript proof.

O my Lord! Let this work of mine be an ongoing charity for myself and for my late parents.

Introduction

By Sheikh Osama Ibrahim Al Haddad, Ph.D.
Imam of Ain Mrayseh Mosque, Beirut
General Inspector, Fatwa Council, Lebanon

In the name of Allah, Most Gracious, Most Merciful

Prayer is a worship that strengthens the individual's tie with his Lord, and this brings him a sense of security. Moreover, it is a worship that can be performed any time, anywhere. When an individual feels the need for help, he just raises his hands and asks it from his Lord.

His prayer will be accepted provided that he does not hasten the response. Prophet Muhammad, peace be upon him, says that one's prayer is answered unless one is in a hurry and complains that he has prayed but his prayer hasn't been answered (narrated by Malik).

This book is about prayer in *The Holy Qur'an*. It presents prayers raised by Allah's prophets, angels, and men and women in general. Those who raise these prayers do so either to glorify Allah the Almighty and win His concern with them, or to ask for all that benefits them in their life or in the Hereafter.

May Allah the Almighty, who hears and responds, make this book beneficial to both its author and readers alike, and may He bless them and bring them plenty in their own life, health, progeny, and knowledge. At last I pray that thanks be to Allah, Lord of all worlds, and may He bless Prophet Muhammad and his family and all his companions.

Preface

Asking for help from God is an act of worship in Islam. It is called prayer, or du'a in Arabic. Allah, the name of God in this Faith, responds to prayer. He encourages the readers of His Book, *The Holy Qur'an*, to call on Him, and He will respond. Prophet Muhammad, peace be upon him (pbuh), says that prayer is the core of worship.

Prayer has a prominent place in *The Holy Qur'an*. There are prayers in it from the beginning to the end.

I classified these prayers into six groups. The first group consists of the prayers that Allah ordered Prophets to say; the second, the prayers that Allah ordered people to say; the third, the prayers raised by angels; the fourth, the prayers raised by Prophets; the fifth, the prayers raised by Believers; and the sixth, the prayers raised by Unbelievers. The two numbers separated by a colon inside brackets in the main text of this book are respectively the chapter's number in *The Holy Qur'an* and that of the prayer's verse.

I followed each prayer with a description of the circumstances in which it was raised, the details of which I took from verses neighbouring that of the prayer and from commentators' notes.

It should be noted that in *The Holy Qur'an,* the word Muslim means one who has submitted his will to that of Allah and not only to a follower of Prophet Muhammad (pbuh).

CHAPTER I

Prayers Allah
Ordered Prophets to Say

Allah ordered Prophet Noah (pbuh) to say that praise be to Allah, and that his disembarking be with Allah's Blessing.

Allah ordered Prophet Muhammad (pbuh) to invite polytheists and their beloved ones to join him and his beloved ones in supplication, and both sides to invoke the curse of Allah on those who say falsehood about Prophet Jesus Christ (pbuh).

Allah also ordered Prophet Muhammad (pbuh) to pray that his entry to the city of Al Madinah be by the Gate of Truth and Honour, and that his exit from Makkah be by the same manner.

Finally, Allah ordered Prophet Muhammad (pbuh) to pray Him for the authority he needed; for praise to be to Him; for enabling him to magnify Allah for His greatness and glory; for increasing him in knowledge; for judgment between him and those who refused Allah's Message; for putting him not among the people who did wrong; and for refuge from the mischief of Darkness and the mischief from people who blew on knots, the mischief from those who were envious, and the mischief from the Whisperers of Evil among Jinns and Men.

Prayers Allah Ordered Prophet Noah (pbuh) to Say

Say O my Lord!
Praise be to Allah

Say O my Lord!
Enable me to disembark with Your Blessing

The people of Prophet Noah (pbuh) did not believe in the oneness of Allah, nor in the Day of Judgment, or in life after death. From among them, Allah chose Noah to be His Messenger to them.

Noah (pbuh) told his people that he carried a message from Allah, ordering him to be a warner to them, and to tell them that unless they become the servants of Allah alone, he would fear for them a grievous day.

The dignitaries among his people did not believe that he had a divine message. They said they saw nothing in him other than a man like themselves, and that those who would follow him were only the meanest among them. They added that he and his followers were liars, not at all deserving to be ranked above them.

Noah (pbuh) did not give up. He went on with his errand, talking to his people with words of love and humility. He said that his message was one of mercy from Allah, and that if this message was obscured from their sight, or if they were averse to it, they were not compelled to accept it. He also made it clear to them that he was not asking for any favours from them, for his reward was from none but Allah, and that he was not going to drive away those who believed him, for they certainly were going to meet their Lord, and then it would become clear as to who were the ignorant ones, those who believed him or those who did not.

The Unbelievers resisted Prophet Noah's mission (pbuh) for human motives. They were jealous of him. So they ignored his superiority. They looked down on the weak and lowly, for they were often better intellectually. They could not believe in what their inferiors in social life believed in, nor could they do what these fellows did.

Moreover, they said that they had never heard that their ancestors believed such a thing as Noah (pbuh) said, arguing that if Allah had wished to send messengers, He could have sent down angels. Finally, they called Noah (pbuh) a mad man, and said that it would be better to leave him alone.

The people of Prophet Noah (pbuh) were given one opportunity after another to do the right thing. Few accepted him as the Messenger of Allah and believed in Allah's oneness, in resurrection, and in life after death. The majority did not. They rejected every advice, haughtily and in disdain.

Prophet Noah (pbuh) asked his Lord to help him overcome their accusation of falsehood.

At Allah's order, Noah (pbuh) built a heavy vessel that would carry the righteous on board and would resist destruction in a sea storm.

There came a flood at the will of Allah, and all the people on land were annihilated. Those who were on board with Noah were saved.

After the Flood, when calm prevailed and Noah was settled under the clear, blue sky, Allah gave him the following order: "Say, Oh my Lord! Praise be to Allah, Who saved us from the wrong-doers (23:28)." 23 is the chapter number in The Holy Book, and 28 is that of the prayer verse.

When the time for disembarkation came, Allah ordered him

to raise the following prayer: "O my Lord! Enable me to disembark with Your Blessing, for You are the best to enable us to disembark (23:29)."

Noah (pbuh), his family, and his followers came down safely from the ship. They truly had sought Allah's light and guidance, so they deserved His grace.

Prayers Allah Ordered
Prophet Muhammad (pbuh) to Say

Say to polytheists: come together with your beloved ones and join me and my beloved ones in supplication, and we together invoke the curse of Allah on those who say falsehood about Jesus Christ

Allah told Prophet Muhammad (pbuh) in *The Holy Qur'an* the story below about the birth and death of Prophet Jesus Christ (pbuh), so that he would be able to refute the false claims made about him.

The angels brought the news to Mary that Allah had chosen her above all women and purified her, and that she was to worship the Lord devoutly, that is, to prostrate herself, and bow down in prayer with those who bow down.

The angels also brought Mary the happy news of a Word from Allah that she would give birth to a boy whose name would be Jesus Christ, the Son of Mary, and that he would be held in honour in this world and the Hereafter. He would speak to the people in childhood and in maturity, and he would be righteous.

Mary asked her Lord in astonishment, how could it be that she would have a son when no man had touched her. Allah said, even so. Allah creates what He wills. When He has decreed a matter, He but says to it, 'Be', and it is!

Allah would teach Jesus (pbuh) the Torah and the Gospel, and appoint him Messenger to Prophet Jacob's descendants, referred to in *The Holy Qur'an* as the Children of Israel. His Message to them was the following: "I have come to you with a sign from your Lord, in that I make for you out of clay, as it were the figure of a bird, and breathe into it, and it becomes a bird by Allah's leave; and I heal those born blind, and the lepers, and I bring the dead into life by Allah's leave; and I declare openly what you eat, and what you store in your houses.

"Surely therein is a sign for you if you do believe. I have come to you, to attest the Torah, which was in existence before me, and to make lawful to you part of what was before forbidden to you; I have come to you with a sign from your Lord. So fear Allah and obey me."

Allah also told Prophet Muhammad (pbuh) to say to those who would wonder that Jesus was born without a human father that Adam was also so born, indeed he was born without either a human father or mother.

A Christian delegation came to Prophet Muhammad (pbuh) in Al Madinah from Najran, a region along the border with Yemen. They were so much impressed on hearing verses from *The Holy Qur'an*, explaining the position of Jesus Christ. They had entered into tributary relations with the new Muslim State, but ingrained habits and customs prevented them from accepting Islam as a religion.

Allah ordered Prophet Muhammad (pbuh) to say the following to those who disputed the position of Jesus Christ (pbuh) with him: "Come! Let us gather together, our sons and your sons, our women and your women, ourselves and yourselves, then let us earnestly pray, and invoke the curse of

Allah on those who lie (3:61)!"

The delegation from Najran declined the invitation.

Say O my Lord! Let my entry be by the Gate of Truth and Honour, and my exit be by the Gate of Truth and Honour; and grant me from You an authority to aid me

The enemies of Prophet Muhammad (pbuh) offered to give him wealth and position among them if he only promised to respect their idols. They tried to tempt him away from that which Allah had revealed to him, and to substitute in the name of Allah something quite different.

Allah told His Prophet in *The Holy Qur'an* that their purpose was to scare him away from the land, and that he would have inclined to them a little had Allah not given him strength. Allah told him also that their attempt was no new thing in the history of the ungodly with His Messengers, and that Allah protects His own.

Allah ordered Muhammad (pbuh) to establish five daily acts of prostration, called prayers, so as to have Allah's aid. These prayers are one in the early morning, called Fajr, and four from the declination of the sun from the zenith to the fullest darkness of the night, respectively called Zuhr, immediately after the sun begins to decline in the afternoon; 'Asr, in the late afternoon; Maghrib, immediately after sunset; and Isha, after the glow of sunset has disappeared and the full darkness of the night has set in.

Muhammad (pbuh) performed these five canonical prayers, and he performed, in addition, a prayer called The Tahajjud, which he did after midnight, in the short hours of the morning.

At Allah's order, he said, "O my Lord! Let my entry be by

the Gate of Truth and Honour, and my exit be by the Gate of Truth and Honour; and grant me from You an authority to aid me (17:80)."

This prayer is interpreted as follows: Ask Allah that your departure from Makkah to Al Madinah be understood as coming from pure motives of truth and spiritual honour, and not from motives of anger against the city or its persecution, and that Allah grants you His authority to aid you in your mission.

Say praise be to Allah, Who begets no son, and has no partner in His dominion, nor needs He any to protect Him from humiliation; and magnify Him for His greatness and glory

The Holy Qur'an in its primary form was revealed verbally to Prophet Muhammad (pbuh). Allah says in it that it was He Who sent it down, and that it was not forged by anyone, nor was it falsified or corrupted in the process of being communicated to mankind.

Allah revealed it in parts, one at a time, so that the Prophet (pbuh) might recite it to people at intervals. When it was recited to those who were given knowledge beforehand, they would fall down on their faces in humble prostration, glorifying their Lord. It satisfied their spiritual yearnings.

Allah sent His Messengers to give glad tidings to believers and a warning to sinners. This was the mission of Prophet Muhammad (pbuh), too. The ungodly's rejection of Allah's Message was not his responsibility.

Allah ordered Muhammad (pbuh) to say, "Praise be to Allah, Who begets no son, and has no partner in His dominion, nor needs He any to protect Him from humiliation; Yea, magnify Him for His greatness and glory (17:111)!"

Muhammad (pbuh) was also ordered to say a prayer of praise in the following situations:

Allah is well acquainted with all that people do. Those who do good will be rewarded in the Hereafter. They will be secure from the terror of the Day of Judgment. Those who do evil will be thrown headlong into the Fire.

Muhammad (pbuh) made it clear to everybody that he was commanded to serve Allah, and to be one of those who bow in Islam to Allah's Will.

He rehearsed *The Holy Qur'an* in Makkah. Those who accepted guidance did so for the good of their own souls.

Allah ordered him to say to those who rejected it, "I am only a warner", and to say, "Praise be to Allah, Who will soon show you His Signs, so that you shall know them (27:92–93)."

Allah told the Prophet (pbuh) that He was not unmindful of all that he and his followers did. Their patient endurance and constancy with which they met persecution and exile were all known to Him, and He would reward them for all of that.

Muhammad (pbuh) was ordered to say a prayer of praise also when Allah told him about people to whom His goodness was clear by rain and the other gifts of nature, and by the daily and seasonal changes which made life so reviving.

Allah told him (pbuh) that if he asked these people whether they knew who gave life to the earth, they would reply that it was Allah. Allah ordered him to say, "Praise be to Allah (29:63)!"
Say increase me in knowledge

The Holy Qur'an unfolds its meaning and purpose gradually to any given individual. No one should be impatient about it.

It explains some warnings, in order that people may take care. Evil people are warned that they may repent, while good people are confirmed in their faith.

Believers are aware that they need knowledge from Allah and His Messenger. They want to be sure they are on the right way of life, in order that they get Allah's reward.

Allah ordered Prophet Muhammad (pbuh) to say. "O my Lord! Increase me in knowledge (20:114)." Believers take it that this prayer is for them also to raise.

People who turn away from Allah will have a rude awakening when the Judgment Day comes. On that day, the loud blast of the Trumpet will be heard, and there will be the stillness and hush of awe and reverence.

The falsehoods of this life that corrupt people found so attractive, will be a grievous burden to them that day. On the other hand, those who worked deeds of righteousness, and had faith, will have no fear of harm. They will be rewarded to the full.

Say O my Lord! Judge in truth between me and those who refuse Your Message

Allah sent Prophet Muhammad (pbuh) to be a mercy for all people, and *The Holy Qur'an* is a message for those who would truly worship Allah.

The Message of Allah impartially teaches all how to carry out Allah's Will and live a good life.

There will be among those who will accept the Message, people who will feel aggrieved that those outside it are better off from a worldly point of view. Allah ordered Prophet Muhammad (pbuh) to tell these people that the fleeting enjoyment of this world's goods is but a trial, and they should be grateful for being saved from temptation.

Allah also ordered him to tell his people that he was ordered by inspiration to convey the following to them: Their God is One God, called Allah; they are to bow to Allah's Will in the Faith of Islam; he proclaims Allah's Message to all alike; and he does not know whether the Day of Judgment is near or far.

If they refused to listen, he was ordered to say, "O my Lord! Judge You in truth (21:112)." Allah's judgment will be the true one.

Say O my Lord! Put me not among the people who do wrong

Every time a messenger came to a people, they accused him of falsehood. Their punishment was that they were wiped out, habitation and all. The following are some examples.

Prophet Hud (pbuh) was sent to a people called 'Ad. He asked them to worship Allah alone and not to worship their idols. They refused to do so, saying that Hud (pbuh) was either a liar or a fool. Allah punished them with a curse.

Prophet Salih (pbuh) was sent to a people called Thamud. He asked them to worship Allah, their Creator. They told him that they would not give up worshipping what their fathers had worshipped. And they refused to give the poor and a she-camel their right to graze on common lands. For their defiance, Allah punished them with a terrible earthquake.

Allah sent Prophet Moses (pbuh) and his brother Aaron to Pharaoh and his chiefs. But these did not believe in them. They wondered arrogantly how they were to believe in two men as Messengers of Allah, whose people were subject to them. They were punished by being drowned in the sea.

The people of Prophet Muhammad (pbuh) did wrong to him. Their leaders disobeyed him. They showed no faith in what he said. When the verses of *The Holy Qur'an* were recited to them, they turned back on their heels, talking nonsense about what they heard. They said it was like one telling fables by night for amusement, and accused Prophet Muhammad (pbuh) of being possessed, though they had known him so well long before his mission, and had called him the truthful.

They denied the Messenger not because they did not recognize him, but because he had brought the Truth to them, which most of them hated. They saw in it a threat to their interests.

Allah told Prophet Muhammad (pbuh) that they would be punished, not only on the Day of Judgment, but also in this very life when the time comes for punishment, and He ordered him to say the following prayer: "O my Lord! If you will show me in my lifetime that which they are warned against, then, O my Lord, put me not among the people who do wrong (23:93–94)!"

Allah's chastisement befalls wrong-doers rather than His Messengers to them. In ordering Prophet Muhammad (pbuh) to raise this prayer, Allah provides him with an opportunity to show his humility to His Lord.

Say I seek refuge with my Lord from all mischief

People in general are afraid of the darkness of the night and of other evils, like injuries, accidents, and calamities.

They are also afraid of witchcraft, especially of a form of it called blowing on knots, which is practised by perverted women, who do secret plottings, display seductive charms, and spread rumours to frighten men.

Another evil in this life is malignant envy, which may destroy the happiness enjoyed by other people.

Evil manifests itself in secret whispers within the

individual's own heart, so as to sap his will. It whispers and then withdraws, to make its work the more subtle and alluring.

Allah is the Lord, Maker, and Cherisher of mankind. He sustains everybody and cares for them. Therefore an individual seeks Allah's protection against evil. The best guard against evil is trust in Allah and taking refuge in divine guidance.

Allah ordered Prophet Muhammad (pbuh) to raise this prayer, "Say I seek refuge with the Lord of the Dawn, from the mischief of created things; from the mischief of Darkness as it overspreads; from the mischief of those who blow on knots; and from the mischief of the envious one as he practises envy (113:1–5)."

This prayer invokes protection against external factors which might affect an individual. In another prayer, Allah orders Prophet Muhammad (pbuh) for protection from internal factors. It is the following: "Say I seek refuge with the Lord and Cherisher of mankind, the King of mankind, the God of mankind from the mischief of the whisperer of evil among jinns and men, who whispers into the hearts of mankind, and withdraws after his whisper (114:1-6)."

CHAPTER II

Prayers Allah Ordered People to Say

Allah ordered the people of Prophet Moses (pbuh) to remember His favours to them, and to be humble and pray Him for His forgiveness.

Allah ordered the people of Prophet Muhammad (pbuh) to ask Him for His forgiveness on their way back from Mount 'Arafat, while doing their pilgrimage.

Allah ordered grown-up children to ask Him to bestow His mercy on their parents.

Finally, Allah ordered people in general to raise prayer to Him.

A Prayer Allah Ordered the People of Prophet Moses (pbuh) to Say

Say forgive us and We shall forgive you your faults, and increase the share of sustenance to those who do good

Allah ordered the people of Moses (pbuh) to remember His special favours to them, and to remember His preferring them to all others. Allah also told them to be on their guard, for special favours did not exempt them from the personal responsibility of each one of them.

The special favours of Allah to Moses' people (pbuh) included the following: Allah saved them from Pharaoh, who had slaughtered their male children and kept their females alive for service. Allah drowned Pharaoh's people in front of their eyes. Allah forgave them for having taken a calf for worship in Moses' absence.

These favours also included the Scripture Allah had given to Moses (pbuh) so that they would know what was right and what was wrong.

They ignored these favours, and said, "O Moses! We shall never believe in you until we see Allah manifestly."

Thereupon a thunderbolt seized them.

Allah raised them up after their death, and His favours to them were resumed. He gave them the shade of clouds to protect them from sunburn in the desert, and sent down to them a food called manna and a bird called quail.

Moreover, Allah gave them entry to a town rich in fruits, just east of the Jordan River, telling them to enter the gate prostrating, and to say a word Allah ordered them to say, which implied humility, and to pray Him for forgiveness. Allah added that if they did that in obedience, He would forgive them for their faults and increase the portion of sustenance to those who did good (2:58).

But they changed the word Allah had ordered them to say, namely *Hittatun*, which meant 'O Our Lord! Take our sins off our shoulders'. They said *Hintatun* instead, which meant wheat. And they entered the gate on their buttocks, not prostrating as they were ordered.

Their defiance did not cease, thus harming not Him, but their own selves, according to Allah.

A Prayer Allah Ordered the People of Prophet Muhammad (pbuh) to Say

Ask for Allah's forgiveness

Allah ordered The people of Prophet Muhammad (pbuh) performing their pilgrimage, what to do and what not to do during this worship.

The pilgrims should abstain from obscenity, wickedness, and wrangling; take a provision with them for the journey, knowing that the best of provisions was right conduct, which emerged from the fear of Allah; buy and sell, making sure that their trade met the interests of both the trader and the community, and that the income from it should be seen as profit from the bounty of Allah. This last order was meant to tell them that honest trade was a form of service to the community and therefore to Allah.

They should wear a simple, white garment in two pieces of unsewn clothes. The wearing of this garment was to be done at certain points definitely fixed on all the roads to Makkah. They should not wear other clothes until the end of the pilgrimage. Nor should they wear ornaments or perfume, nor should they anoint their hair, or go hunting.

The pilgrims should walk around the Ka'ba seven times, and follow this with a short prayer at the Station of Abraham. Then they should walk from Safa to Marwa and back to Safa a definite number of times.

They should listen to an exposition of the meaning of pilgrimage on the seventh day of this worship's month; go to the Valley of Mina on the eighth day and stay the night there; proceed on the ninth day to the plain and hill of 'Arafat and raise their prayers to Allah all day.

On their way back from 'Arafat, they should celebrate the praises of Allah at a place called Muzdalifah then, as they continued their way back to Mina, they were ordered to ask for Allah's forgiveness (2:199). Allah would respond, for He is often forgiving and most merciful.

On the tenth day of the month, they should stay in the valley of Mina for prayer and praise. This is the 'Id Day, the day for giving sacrifice.

After offering the sacrifice, they should shave their heads or trim their hair, cast seven pebbles at the Jamarat, and continue casting pebbles on subsequent days. This casting of pebbles symbolized the rejection of evil.

Finally they should walk around the Ka'ba seven times, called tawaf al-Ifada. This was the completion rite of the pilgrimage.

A Prayer Allah Ordered Grown-up Children to Say

Say my Lord! Bestow Your mercy on my parents

Allah had decreed that children should be kind to their parents. Whether one or both parents attain old age in their child's lifetime, the child should not say a word of contempt, nor repel them but address them in terms of honour.

Grown-up children should pray for their parents. Allah ordered them to say: "My Lord, bestow on them Your mercy even as they cherished me in my childhood (17:24)."

In early childhood, when the parents were strong and the child was helpless, parental affection was showered on the child. When the child grew up and was strong, and the parents were helpless, could he do less than bestow similar tender care on his parents?

He should lower to them the wing of humility like a high-flying bird lowers its wing out of tenderness to its offspring. This metaphor suggests that parental love should be a type of divine love, that is, more than human gratitude. Nothing that he can do can ever really compensate for that which he has received.

A Prayer Allah Ordered People in General to Say

"And your Lord says, 'Call on Me; I will answer your prayer. But those who are too arrogant to worship Me, will surely enter Hell abased (40:60)'."

Allah orders people to ask for help from Him, and He will answer their prayer in the following way: He may give the help He is asked for at once, or He may delay it, or He may substitute it.

Those who did not worship Him, would certainly go to hell humiliated.

Allah ordered Prophet Muhammad (pbuh) to tell those who pray for help, that Allah is indeed close to them, and that He does listen to their prayer. Allah also ordered him to encourage his followers to obey Allah and to believe in Him, so that the road they walk be the right one.

Prophets knew that Allah listened to prayer. Prophet Zakariya (pbuh), for example, before his son Yahya was born, prayed his Lord for a progeny that was pure, and added that Allah was the One Who Heard prayer. Another example is Prophet Abraham (pbuh). After Ismail and Isaac were born, he said that his Lord was the Hearer of prayer.

But prayer without faith is delusion. Those in the Fire will pray Allah to lighten for them the torture of Hell for a day. The Keepers of Hell will ask them whether or not Allah's Messengers came to them with Clear Signs from Him. They will answer in the affirmative. The Keepers will reply that the prayer of those without faith is nothing but futile wandering.

CHAPTER III

Prayers of Angels

Angels pray that praise be to Allah, that repentants be forgiven and preserved from the Fire and from all ills. They also pray that the righteous among repentants, their fathers, their wives, and their posterity be given entry to Paradise.

Praise be to Allah

The angels surrounding the Divine Throne, sing Glory and Praise to their Lord. They thank Allah for His perfect justice on the Day of Judgment, when the believers and the unbelievers are both given what they were promised. The angels say, "Praise be to Allah, the Lord of the Worlds (39:75)!"

Forgiveness for repentants and preservation from the chastisement of the blazing Fire

Entry for repentants to the Gardens of Eternity, together with the righteous among their fathers, wives, and posterity

Preservation of repentants from all ills

The Angels who bear the Throne of Allah and those around it, implore forgiveness for repentants. They pray Allah, Who embraces all things in Mercy and Knowledge, to forgive those who turn in repentance and follow His Path, and to preserve them from the chastisement of the blazing Fire.

Moreover, they pray to Allah to grant repentants and the righteous among their fathers, their wives, and their posterity entry to the Gardens of Eternity, which He has promised to them. The Angels do that, asserting that Allah is exalted in might and full of wisdom. They finally ask Him to preserve repentants from all ills, for any whom He does preserve from ills that day, will have indeed the highest achievement (40:7–9).

CHAPTER IV

Prayers of Prophets

Adam (pbuh) asked Allah for forgiveness to him and to his wife.

Noah (pbuh) asked Allah for judgment between him and the unbelievers, and for safety from them. He also asked Allah to help him against those who accused him of falsehood, and not to leave on earth a single one of the unbelievers. Moreover, he asked forgiveness for himself, his parents, all believers, and all those who entered his house and were in faith. He also prayed that the wrong-doers be granted an increase in perdition. Finally, he asked for excuse from Allah for having asked Him about his son, which was not his right to ask.

An anonymous prophet (pbuh) asked for help against accusers among his people.

Abraham (pbuh) asked for a righteous progeny; for security to the city of Makkah; for visits by believers to this city; for food and drink to its inhabitants; for guidance to them to do regular prayer; and for forgiveness to his parents and all believers. For himself, he asked for useful knowledge and righteous work; for a good name and for a praise lasting to the Day of Judgment; for residence in Paradise; and for acceptance of his and his son Ismail's construction of Allah's House in Makkah.

Lut (pbuh) asked for the rescue of his people from vice.

Joseph (pbuh) asked for resistance against temptation.

Shu'aib (pbuh) asked for Allah's judgment between him and

his people.

Job (pbuh) asked for the removal of distress and a remedy from Satan's afflictions.

Moses (pbuh) asked for safety from a rebellious people; for defacement of the arrogant's wealth; and for forgiveness, having asked for a look at Allah, presumably a thing nobody was allowed to ask for.

David (pbuh), having thought that he had overlooked for a moment Allah's grace to him, asked for His forgiveness.

Solomon (pbuh) asked for Allah's forgiveness for having been overwhelmed by his power, and for a kingdom never to be granted to anyone after him.

Jonah (pbuh) asked for acceptance of his repentance.

Zakariya (pbuh) asked for an heir and a pure progeny.

Jesus Christ (pbuh) asked for a table for his followers, set with choice foods.

Muhammad (pbuh) asked for assistance in battle.

Prophet Adam (pbuh)

To forgive him and his wife

Allah ordered Adam (pbuh) to dwell with his wife Eve in the Garden of Comfort and Bliss, and to enjoy its good things. He was also ordered not to approach a tree that Allah signaled to him, lest they, Adam and Eve, become of the unjust. They were warned of the danger implicit in that order.

Satan whispered suggestions to them. His purpose was to reveal to them their body parts that were hidden from them and were shameful to reveal. He told them that their Lord had forbidden them that tree to prevent them from becoming angels or such beings that live forever. He swore to them that he was their sincere adviser.

They tasted the fruit of the tree, disobeying Allah's order. Their shameful parts became manifest to them, and they began to sew together the leaves of the Garden over their bodies.

So by deceit, Satan brought about their fall.

Their Lord called unto them, "Did I not forbid you that tree, and tell you that Satan was an avowed enemy unto you?"

Allah ordered them to get down to earth, which will be their dwelling place and their means of livelihood during their lifetime. On it, they and their progeny will live and die, and from it, they will be taken out on the Day of Judgment.

Adam and Eve said, "Our Lord! We have wronged our own souls. If You forgive us not and bestow not upon us Your Mercy, we shall certainly be lost (7:23)."

Adam received an inspiration that Allah's Grace responded to his (and his wife's) effort for an excuse, and his Lord turned towards him, for He is Oft-Returning, Most Merciful. There will come to Adam's progeny Guidance from Allah, and for those who follow His Guidance, there shall be no fear, nor shall they grieve.

Prophet Noah (pbuh)

To judge openly between him and the unbelievers, and to save him and the believers from them

The people of Prophet Noah (pbuh) had rejected Allah's messengers before he was sent to them. They had lost all faith and abandoned themselves to evil.

Noah (pbuh) was one of them. They knew him well. He was

pure in heart and conduct.

He (pbuh) advised them to fear Allah, to lead righteous lives and to keep away from evil. He assured them that he was to them a trustworthy messenger, and requested them to obey him. He told them that he would not ask for any reward from them, and repeated his advice to them to fear Allah.

They argued that they would not believe him when it was the meanest among them were his followers. Noah (pbuh) told them that he would not judge the individuals to whom they referred because he did not know what they did, adding that only Allah would judge them. He (pbuh) further explained that he was sent only as a plain warner, and he was not one to drive away those who believed.

The unbelievers warned Noah (pbuh) that unless he stopped what he was doing, he would be stoned to death.

Noah (pbuh) complained to Allah that his people had rejected him, and implored Him, saying, "Judge you, then, between me and them openly, and deliver me and the believers who are with me (26:118)."

Allah delivered him and the believers.

To help him against those who accused him of falsehood

Noah (pbuh) spoke to his people kindly, advising them to worship Allah and to show that they fear Him.

The chiefs of his people told everybody that Noah was no more than a man like themselves, and that his wish was to assert his superiority over them. They added that Allah could have sent down angels if He had wished to send messengers, and that they had never heard among their ancestors such a thing as he said.

They also thought Noah (pbuh) was mad and advised people

that it would be better to leave him alone.

Noah (pbuh) said, "O my Lord! Help me. They accuse me of falsehood (23:26)!"

Allah inspired him to build a ship and to wait for His command.

To help him against those who rejected him

The people of Prophet Noah (pbuh) rejected him. They drove him out, saying that he was possessed.

He called on his Lord: "I am one overcome. Do You then help me (54:10)!"

Allah bore him together with his family and followers, on a ship made of broad planks and caulked with palm-fibre. The ship floated under Allah's eyes and care, as a reward to one who had been rejected with scorn.

Allah opened the gates of heaven with water pouring forth. And He caused the earth to gush forth with springs. So the waters met and rose to the extent decreed, causing a huge flood which inundated the country.

Not to leave of the unbelievers a single one on earth

To forgive him, his parents, all believing men and believing women, and all who enter his house in faith, and to give the wrong-doers no increase but in perdition

Noah (pbuh) observed that the unbelievers followed rich men, who advised them not to abandon their gods Wadd, Suwa, Yaguth, Ya'uq, and Nasr. He complained to Allah that they and their followers had already misled many.

He said, "O my Lord! Leave not of the unbelievers a single

one on earth (71:26)!" He feared that if Allah did leave any of them, they would mislead believers, and would breed none but ungrateful people.

Allah answered his prayer. The unbelievers were drowned in the Flood.

The prayer of Noah (pbuh) was not vindictive. It simply meant that he asked that the roots of sin be cut off.

He also prayed for forgiveness to himself, to his parents, and to all believers, not only in his own age but in all ages to come, and in all places. He said, "O my Lord! Forgive me, my parents, all who enter my house in faith, and all believing men and believing women." To the wrong-doers, he prayed Allah to give them nothing but an increase in perdition (71:28).

To forgive him and give him mercy

Noah (pbuh) had all the believers with him on board the ship, who were only a few.

He made it clear to them that they had embarked in the name of Allah, whether the ship was on the move or at rest. He assured them that his Lord was Oft-Forgiving, Most Merciful.

While everybody was getting on board, he called out to his son, inviting him to embark with them and not to be with the unbelievers. The son replied that he would betake himself to some mountain which would save him from the water. The young man thought he would be safe on a mountain peak, not knowing that all peaks would be submerged. Noah (pbuh) said that nothing could save any from the Command of Allah except those on whom He has mercy.

The ship sailed. The waves were mountain high. Noah's son was among those who were drowned.

Allah ordered the earth to swallow up its water, and the sky to withhold its rain. The water abated, the matter ended, and the ship rested on Mount Judi, and the word that went forth was 'away with those who do wrong!'

Allah ordered Noah (pbuh) to come down from the ship with peace from Him and blessing on him and on some of the peoples who would spring from those who were with him. There would be other peoples, Allah told him, to whom He should grant their pleasures for a time, but in the end a grievous chastisement would reach them from Him.

Noah (pbuh) called upon his Lord, saying surely his son was of his family. Allah told him that his son was not of his family, for his conduct was unrighteous, and that he should not ask of Allah that which he had no knowledge of.

Noah said, "O my Lord! I do seek refuge with You from asking You for that of which I have no knowledge, and unless You forgive me and have mercy on me, I should indeed be among the losers (11:47)!"

Allah forgave him.

An Anonymous Prophet

To help him against his accusers of falsehood

The name of the prophet who raised this prayer is not mentioned.

His mission was to preach the message delivered by prophets in general, which went on as follows: "Worship Allah! You have no other god but Him. Will you not fear him?"

Every prophet was maligned and persecuted.

The chiefs of this prophet's people denied the existence of the Hereafter. They said that he was not a prophet, that he was no more than one like themselves, and that he ate and drank of what they ate and drank. They warned their people that if they obeyed him, then it was certain that they would be lost. They rejected his warning that they would be brought forth again after they had died and become dust was meaningless, adding that there was no future life, and that they were not fools to believe such a thing.

The prophet said, "O my Lord help me, for that they accuse me of falsehood (23:39)."

Allah said that in a short while they were to be sorry.

A frightful earthquake came by night and buried them in their own homes.

Prophet Abraham (pbuh)

To grant him a righteous son

The conflict between Prophet Abraham (pbuh) and his people was severe. While they cared more for ancestral custom, he took the side of truth. He could not possibly share in their false beliefs. His father was among the chief supporters of these beliefs. This increased his grief. It was strong on his mind and soul.

His people plotted against him, and his life was in danger. He decided to go to his Lord, Who would surely guide him.

Trusting himself to Allah, he migrated from his land in Iraq to Palestine at the eastern shores of the Mediterranean Sea.

Abraham (pbuh) was already an elderly man, and he felt the need for a son to help him. He prayed Allah to grant him a righteous son (37:100–101). Allah responded to his prayer and Ismail was born.

Ismail's character was forbearing, like that of his father. To both of them self-sacrifice in the service of Allah was the supreme thing in life.

His father told him that he had seen in a dream that he offered him in sacrifice, and asked him to see what his view was. The son told his father to do as he was commanded, and he would find him, if Allah so willed, one of the steadfast.

As Abraham (pbuh) laid Ismail prostrate on his forehead for sacrifice, Allah called out to him, "O Abraham! You have already fulfilled the dream!"

It was a clear trial.

Allah ransomed him with a fine sheep, and with his name to be remembered forever.

To make Makkah a city of peace

Abraham (pbuh) and his son Ismail removed the idols that were in Makkah. They purified it for those who went round the Ka'ba and retired to it for prayer and spiritual practice.

Allah told Abraham (pbuh) by revelation that He would make him an imam, a leader in religion. Abraham asked if there would be imams also from his progeny. Allah answered that His promise was not within the reach of evil-doers.

Makkah lies in a rocky and barren territory.

Abraham (pbuh) said, "My Lord, make this a city of peace, and feed its people with fruits – such of them as believe in Allah and the Last Day (2:126)." His prayer was for those inhabitants of Makkah who believed in Allah and the Day of Judgment.

Allah added that He would grant these pleasures in this life also to those who rejected faith, and in the next life they would go to Hell.

To accept his and his son's raising of the foundations of the

Abraham (pbuh) founded the origins of Islam in Arabia. He cleared out of Makkah all such signs of paganism or star-worship or planet-worship as there were in his time. He and his son Ismail then built the Ka'aba and established the rites and practices of the sacred city.

He dedicated his work to Allah in the following, humble prayer: "Our Lord! Accept this service from us. For you are the All-Hearing, the All-Knowing (2:127)."

Abraham (pbuh) looked forward to winning Allah's mercy. He prayed that he, his son Ismail, and their progeny have faith in Allah.

Allah answered Abraham's prayer. He ordered him to submit his will to Him. Abraham (pbuh) replied that he submitted his will to Allah, the Lord and Cherisher of the Universe.

Abraham (pbuh) told his sons that Allah had chosen the Faith of Islam for them, and added, "Then die not except in the state of submission to Him."

He (pbuh) asked Allah to bring out of his progeny a people of Muslims, that is, a people who would be in the state of submission to Allah. He also asked his Lord to show these Muslims where to celebrate the due rites. He praised Allah as the Oft-Relenting and Most Merciful, and asked Him to be merciful to Muslims.

Abraham's son, Prophet Jacob (pbuh), when death appeared before him, he too said to his sons, "What will you worship after me?" They said, "We shall worship Your God and the God of your fathers – Abraham, Ismail, and Isaac, the one true God. To Him do we submit."

To send the people of Makkah a messenger from among them, who will rehearse Allah's Signs to them

Allah had chosen Prophet Abraham (pbuh) and rendered him in this world pure in heart. In the Hereafter, he will be in the ranks of the righteous.

Abraham (pbuh) raised the following prayer: "Our Lord! Send amongst them a Messenger of their own, who shall rehearse Your Signs to them and instruct them in Scripture and Wisdom, and purify them. For You are the Exalted in Might the Wise (2:129)."

He (pbuh) foresaw in the Ka'ba, the cube-shaped structure that he and his son Ismail had built in the centr of the Sacred Mosque in the city of Makkah, a prophet teaching the people as one of them and in their own Arabic language.

To make him one who will establish regular prayer, and to raise such a person among his offspring who will do the same

To accept his prayer

To cover him with His forgiveness, together with his parents and all believers, on the day when the reckoning will be established

Prophet Abraham (pbuh), having seen that idols had led astray many among mankind, asked Allah to preserve him and his sons from worshipping them. He added that people who followed his ways were of him, while those who disobeyed him were to be left for Allah, Who is indeed Oft-Forgiving, Most Merciful.

Abraham (pbuh) also asked Allah to fill the hearts of some people with love towards his family, whom he had made to dwell in a valley without cultivation, close to Allah's Sacred House, in order to establish regular prayer. Moreover, he asked Allah to feed them with fruits so that they may become thankful to Him. He also asked Allah to accept his prayer, and to forgive him, his parents, and all believers.

Following is his prayer: "O my Lord! Make me one who establishes regular prayer, and also raise such among my offspring. O our Lord! And accept my Prayer. O our Lord! Cover us with Your forgiveness – me, my parents, and all believers, on the day when the reckoning will be established (14:40–41)."

To sing praise to Allah for having granted unto him in old age his two sons Ismail and Isaac

Abraham (pbuh) says, "Praise be to Allah, Who has granted unto me in old age Ismail and Isaac, for truly my Lord is He, the Hearer of Prayer (14:39)!"

Isma'il was born when his father was eighty-six years old and, when he was thirteen and his father ninety-nine, his brother Isaac was born. Both sons were the children of their father's old age, and both were prophets like their father, peace be upon them.

To bestow wisdom on him, and join him with the righteous

To grant him honourable mention on the tongue of truth among the future generations

To make him one of the inheritors of the Garden of Bliss

To forgive his father, who is among those astray, and not to let him be in disgrace on the Day when men will be raised up

Prophet Abraham (pbuh) showed in the form of a prayer what his inmost wishes were. He wanted his own soul enlightened with divine wisdom, his heart and life filled with righteousness. He would not be content with working only for himself or his own generation; his good wishes extended to all future generations.

His prayer is the following: "O my Lord! Bestow wisdom on me, and join me with the righteous; grant me honourable mention on the tongue of truth among the latest generations; make me one of the inheritors of the Garden of Bliss; forgive my father, who is among those astray; and let me not be in disgrace on the Day when men will be raised up, the Day whereon neither wealth nor sons will avail, but he will prosper that brings to Allah a sound heart (26:83–89)."

He (pbuh) prayed for wisdom, righteousness, honourable reputation among future generations; for the Garden of Bliss; for forgiveness to his father so that he would not be disgraced on the Day of Judgment.

Prophet Lut (pbuh)

To protect him and his family from perverse sexual feelings

Prophet Lut (pbuh) was a nephew of Prophet Abraham (pbuh). Allah sent him as a warner to the people of Sodom and Gomorrah, two cities in the plain east of the Dead Sea.

Their deeds astonished him. He asked them how, of all the creatures in the world, they would approach males and leave those whom Allah had created for them to be their mates, and added, "Nay, you are a people transgressing all limits!"

He told them that Allah was worthy of all trust, and encouraged them to fear Him and obey His Messenger.

He explained that he would not ask for a reward from them for his help, as his reward was only from the Lord of the Worlds.

They rejected him as they had rejected the messengers

before him, and threatened to cast him and those who believed in him out if he did not leave them alone. Their warrant was that Prophet Lut (pbuh) and his followers were indeed men who wanted to be clean and pure!

Lut (pbuh) raised the following prayer: "O my Lord! Deliver me and my family from such things as they do (26:169)!" Allah answered his prayer. He rained down on them a shower of brimstone.

Allah delivered Prophet Lut (pbuh) and his family, all except an old woman who lingered behind. This was Lut's wife, whose attitude was to hark back to the glitter of wickedness and sin, in spite of her association with the righteous. She was among those who perished.

Prophet Joseph (pbuh)

To turn seduction attempts away from him

When Joseph (pbuh) was a child, his brothers were jealous of him because their father loved him more than them. They planned to get rid of him so as to have their father's love all to themselves.

They threw him down to the bottom of a well, and after sunset they returned home and told their father that the wolf had eaten their brother, showing him Joseph's shirt stained with false blood. Their father told them that he did not believe their tale, and that he sought patience from Allah.

A caravan of travellers came to the well for water. They found Joseph there and took him out of the well and sold him in Egypt. The man who bought him was the Ruler of that country. He had no children. He asked his wife to make the boy's stay among them honourable.

Joseph attained his full manhood and was extraordinarily handsome. Allah gave him power and knowledge, rewarding him for being one of those who did right.

The woman in whose house Joseph was, fastened the doors and sought to seduce him. He resisted her attempts, saying that her husband was good to him, and deserved gratitude from him.

Ladies in the city said the Ruler's wife sought to seduce her slave. He had inspired her with violent love. "We see," they said, "she is evidently going astray."

When she heard of their malicious talk, she invited them to a banquet, and her servants at her order set the table in front of each woman with fruits and a knife.

She said to Joseph, "Come out before them."

When they saw Joseph, they did extol him, and in their amazement cut their hands. They said, "May Allah Preserve us! No mortal is this! This is none other than a noble angel!"

She said, "There before you is the man about whom you did blame me! I did seek to seduce him from his true self but he did firmly save himself guiltless! And now, if he continues with what he is doing, he shall certainly be cast into prison, and what is more he will be in the company of the vilest!"

Joseph raised the following prayer: "O my Lord! The prison is dearer to my liking than that to which they invite me. Unless You turn their snare away from me, I should feel inclined towards them and join the ranks of the ignorant (12:33)."

His Lord hearkened to him, and turned their snare away from him.

To take his soul at death as one submitting to Allah's will as a Muslim, and unite him with the righteous

The King of Egypt saw in a dream seven fat cows, and seven lean ones devour them; and seven green ears of corn, and seven others withered. He asked his chiefs to interpret this dream to him. They said that they did not know what it meant.

Among those present in the court was the cup-bearer. He asked permission to withdraw in order to find the interpretation.

This man remembered that Joseph knew how to interpret dreams. They had met in prison. Joseph was still there, so he went straight to him, and asked him for an interpretation.

Joseph (pbuh) said that there would be seven years of abundant harvest.

The King ordered that Joseph be brought to him.

Joseph (pbuh) told the messenger to go back to his lord, and tell him that he'd rather clear his case first with the ladies who cut their hands.

The King ordered the ladies to tell him the truth about the whole affair with Joseph. They admitted the truth of his innocence and high principles, and the wife of the Ruler also admitted her own guilt, freely and frankly.

The king told Joseph that as of that day he would be his Minister.

Joseph was given absolute power so that he would be able to carry out an emergency policy that would meet the difficult times of depression.

His reserves met the demands of famine, and Egypt blessed him. The country's harvest was abundant again and people came from neighbouring countries to purchase its corn.

Joseph saw this as one of Allah's favours to him.

Other favours included the arrival of his father and brothers in Egypt, together with their families. His brothers admitted their wrong-doings, and he looked upon them as having been misled by Satan.

He told his father that he saw these favours as a fulfillment of a vision he had seen in childhood.

To Joseph, however, the best reward was the reward of the Hereafter. So he raised to Allah the following prayer: "O my Lord! You have indeed bestowed on me some power, and taught me something of the interpretation of dreams. You are The Creator of the heavens and the earth! You are The Protector in this world and in the Hereafter. Take You my soul at death as one submitting to Your Will as a Muslim, and unite me with the righteous (23:101)." Muslim means one who submits to the will of Allah.

Prophet Shu'aib (pbuh)

To decide in truth between him and his people

Prophet Shu'aib (pbuh) was Allah's Messenger to the Midianites, who lived on the road of merchant caravans between two rich countries, Egypt and Mesopotamia. By Allah's grace they multiplied in numbers and resources. For this they owed a duty to Allah, to obey Him.

Shu'aib (pbuh) told his people that they had no other god but Allah, and advised them to worship Allah. He urged them to obey Allah's orders and give to people just measure and weight, and not to withhold from them the things that were their due, nor to do mischief.

There was internal conflict among Shu'aib's people between those who believed in him and those who did not. As a peace-maker, he ignored the selfish, arrogant motives of those who refused to believe him, and appealed to their better nature and asked them to end their controversies.

He argued that the reason why they suppressed the believers was that they had mental difficulty accepting his mission. He added that events would prove who was right and who was wrong.

Those who believed Prophet Shu'aib (pbuh) and followed his teaching were a minority. He encouraged them to be patient, and to be certain that their faith was strong enough to keep them in the hope that Allah's truth would triumph in the end, and that there was no cause for despair or dejection.

The majority of his people rejected his preaching and threatened to drive him and his followers out of their city, unless they returned to the religion of their fathers.

Shu'aib (pbuh) said that threats would not move him or his followers back to their ancestral religion, adding that he and his followers would only be guided by Allah's will.

The unbelievers threatened Shu'aib's people, too. They said, "If you follow Shu'aib, be sure then you are ruined!" This meant that the believers would be persecuted, their families tortured, and their homes destroyed.

Shu'aib (pbuh) raised the following prayer: "Our Lord! Decide You between us and our people in truth, for You are the best to decide (7:89)."

An earthquake seized the unbelievers by night, and they were buried in their own homes.

Prophet Job (pbuh)

To remove his distress and suffering

Prophet Job (pbuh) suffered from loathsome sores for years, but he never grumbled. He was patient. His wife was not, and she scorned her husband badly.

Job's distress multiplied. He lost his home, his possessions, and his family.

But he was constant in faith.

Years had passed when Prophet Job (pbuh) turned to Allah for help, saying, "Truly distress has seized me, but You are the Most Merciful of those that are merciful (21:83)." He only stated his condition to Allah and praised Him.

Allah commanded him to strike the earth with his foot. He did that and a fountain gushed forth. Job (pbuh) cleaned his body and refreshed his spirits. Then he drank and lay down for some rest.

Allah gave him back his people and doubled their number, as a Grace from Him, and as a thing for commemoration, for all servants of Allah.

Prophet Job (pbuh) has been remembered as an example of dignified patience, ever trustful in Allah.

Prophet Moses (pbuh)

To forgive him for having wronged himself

Moses (pbuh) grew up in Pharaoh's Palace. When he reached full age, he was good at heart and obedient to those among whom he lived.

He had heard that the people who belonged in the city were being oppressed. So he wanted to see for himself how things were going on.

But he was not free to wander about at will in the common quarters of the city, so he entered it at a time, he hoped, when there would be nobody watching.

Moses (pbuh) found there two men fighting, one of the people he belonged to, and the other was an Egyptian. The first man appealed to him against his foe. Moses (pbuh) struck the Egyptian with his fist and the man fell dead.

Moses (pbuh) did not mean to kill the man. He only wanted to release the person who appealed to him.

This was unfortunate to Moses (pbuh), and he was full of regrets and repentance. He said that his deed was a work of Satan, an enemy that manifestly led people to do wrong.

He prayed to Allah, "O my Lord! I have indeed wronged my soul! Do You then forgive me (28:16)?"

Allah forgave him.

Moses (pbuh) took a conscious and solemn vow to dedicate himself to Allah, and to do nothing that may in any way assist those who were doing wrong.

To save him from wrong-doers

In the morning, following the death of the man whom he had struck with his fist, Moses (pbuh) was in the city, fearful and vigilant.

The man who had called him the day before, called aloud for his help again. Exasperated at this public appeal to him, Moses (pbuh) said to him, "Obviously you are given to doing wrong."

After the first day's fight, there was much talk about it in the city, and details of it might have reached the Palace, to which Moses (pbuh) had not dared to return.

A man came to him from the furthest end of the city, and advised him to get away from it, adding that a meeting was held and it was decided to put Moses to death. The man said, "So get you away, for I do give you sincere advice."

Moses (pbuh) saw that his life was not safe anywhere in Pharaoh's territory. He got away from there, looking about, in a state of fear. He did not know where to go.

He prayed, "O my Lord! Save me from people given to wrong-doing (28:21)."

To help him get married

Moses (pbuh) plunged into the Sinai desert, away from Pharaoh's land, hoping that his Lord would show him the right way.

He reached the land of Madyan after a journey that was long and painful. At a watering place there, he saw a group of men watering their flocks. He waited under the shade of a tree until they should finish.

There were two maidens, also waiting with their flocks, which they had come to water.

Moses asked the women what the matter was with them. They said that they could not water their flocks until the shepherds took back their flocks, and explained that their father was an old man. He went at once among the shepherds, made a place at the water for the flocks of the maidens, and went back to his place in the shade.

Moses (pbuh) said: "O my Lord! Truly am I in desperate need of any good that You do send me (28:24)!" It is understood from this prayer that at that moment the idea of having a wife had occurred to Moses.

One of the two maidens came back to him, walking bashfully. She said, "My father invites you so that he may reward you for having watered our flocks for us."

Moses (pbuh) narrated his story to the girl's father, who said,

"Fear you not. Well that you escaped from those who are unjust."

One of the girls asked her father to employ Moses to look after the flocks. She said that he was strong and trusty.

The father asked Moses if he would marry one of his daughters and stay with him for eight or ten years, whichever term he chose. His service for that period was more than sufficient in lieu of a dower.

Moses' heart and that of the girl were mutually attracted. He was glad of the proposal, and accepted it. He said, "Let that be the agreement between me and you. Whichever of the two terms I fulfill, let there be no injustice to me. May Allah be a witness to what we say."

Moses fulfilled the term and left Madyan with his family.

To give him knowledge and affection
To make his mission easy
To remove the defect from his speech
To make his brother Aaron his assistant

Moses (pbuh) was travelling with his family in the Sinai Peninsula when he saw a fire. He asked his wife to wait for him at the place where they were standing, and headed for the fire, saying to her that perhaps he could bring them some burning brand from there or find some guidance.

At the fire he was called by his name, and the Caller told him that He was his Lord, and asked him to put off his shoes (a mark of respect) because he was in the sacred valley Tuwa. Allah told him that He had chosen him to be His Messenger, and ordered him to listen to Him.

Allah said, "Verily, I am Allah. There is no god except me. So serve you me only, and establish regular prayer for my remembrance. Verily the Hour (that is, the Day of Judgment) is coming. I have almost kept it hidden, for every soul to receive its reward by the measure of its endeavor. Therefore let not those who do not believe in me, and follow their own lust instead, divert you from me, lest you perish!"

Allah asked Moses what he carried in his hand. Moses said it was his rod, on which he leant, with which he beat down fodder for his flocks, and in it he found other uses.

Allah said, "Throw it, O Moses!"

He threw it, and to his astonishment, it was a snake, active in motion. Allah ordered him to seize it and not to fear. He at once would return it to its former condition. Moses saw by this demonstration how a miracle worked; it changed the rod's condition.

The rod was the first miracle.

Allah said, "Now draw your hand close to your side. It shall come forth white and shining."

The hand shone as with a divine light.

This was the second miracle.

Allah ordered Moses: "Go you to Pharaoh, for he has indeed transgressed all bounds."

Moses (pbuh) said, "O my Lord! Expand me my breast; ease my task for me; and remove the impediment from my speech, so they may understand what I say. And give me a minister from my family, Aaron, my brother. Add to my strength through him. And make him share my task, so that we may celebrate Your praise and remember You without stint, for You are ever seeing (20:25–35)."

Moses (pbuh) submitted to Allah's order, and asked for His help. First, he prayed for the expansion of his breast, which is reputed to be the seat of knowledge and affection. He then asked for Allah's help in his task. He asked for the removal of the defect from his speech and for the counsel and constant attendance of his brother, Aaron.

Allah said, "Granted is your prayer, O Moses!"

To separate him and his brother from people disobedient to them

Moses (pbuh) asked his people earnestly to remember the favours of Allah to them. He said that Allah chose individuals from among them to be prophets, made those who obeyed Him and followed His Messengers free from slavery, and gave them what He had not given to others.

He asked them to enter the Holy Land, which Allah had assigned to them, and warned them not to turn back, for then they would be overthrown to their own ruin.

They refused to enter the land, saying the people in it were of exceeding strength. They told Moses (pbuh) to turn those people out of the land, and then they would enter it. They were not willing to fight for what they wished to enjoy.

A number of Moses' people who had faith and courage went to that land to inspect it. Two of them returned. They pleaded for an immediate entry after taking due preparations and putting their trust in Allah for victory.

Moses' people ignored what they heard from these two men, and again they said that they refused to enter the land as long as its people were in it. They told him to go together with his Lord and fight while they sat there.

He said, "O my Lord! I have power only over myself and my brother. So separate us from these rebellious people (5:25)!"

Allah said that the land would therefore be out of their reach for forty years, and that they would wander in distraction through the wilderness. "But sorrow you not over these rebellious people," Allah said to Moses.

To show Himself to him

Moses (pbuh) lived on the mount alone apart from his people for forty nights before he took up his ministry. He did this at Allah's order. He had charged his brother Aaron to act for him and to do right, and not to follow the way of those who did mischief.

He raised the following prayer as he was listening to his Lord: "O my Lord! Show Yourself to me, that I may look upon You (7:143)." Allah told him by no means could he see Him, and ordered him to look at the mount nearby. If it abode in its place, then he would see Him.

Allah manifested Himself to the mount. Immediately it broke up into dust, and Moses (pbuh) fell down in a swoon. When he recovered his senses, he said: "Glory be to You! To You I turn in repentance and I am the first to believe." Moses (pbuh) at once repented. The word 'first' here meant most zealous in faith, not the first in time.

Allah answered Moses' prayer with mercy and compassion, telling him that He had chosen him above his contemporaries for the messages He had given him and the words He had spoken to him.

To forgive him and his brother and admit them to His mercy

While Moses (pbuh) was on Mount Sinai, his people below were so ungrateful that they forgot Allah and made a golden calf for worship. They had melted all their ornaments, and made the image of a calf. It produced what they imagined to be a lowing sound, but they did not see that it could neither speak to them, nor show them right from wrong.

When Moses (pbuh) came back to his people, he told them that what they had done in his absence was evil. Their lapse into idolatry had only hastened Allah's wrath. He also told them that he wished they had only waited, for he was bringing to them in the Tablets, the commands of Allah, in the most excellent teaching.

Angry and grieved, he put down the Tablets, turned to his brother Aaron and seized him by the hair of his head, and dragged him.

Moses (pbuh) was but human. His grievance at the turn events had taken was unbearable. He laid his hands on his brother, and his brother at once explained. Full of tenderness and regret, he said, "Son of my mother! The people did indeed reckon me as naught, and went near to slaying me! Make not the enemies rejoice over my misfortune, nor count you me among the people of sin."

Aaron's tender words turned Moses' anger to gentleness. He was convinced that his brother was guiltless. He prayed, "O my Lord! Forgive me and my brother! Admit us to Your mercy! For You are the Most Merciful of those who show mercy (7:151)!"

To forgive him and his followers
To give them His mercy
To ordain for them that which is good in this life and in the Hereafter

Moses (pbuh) took seventy of the elders among his people to repent for having worshipped the calf, to a place at some distance from the Mount where Allah had spoken to him.

The faith of these older people, however, was not yet complete. They dared to say to Moses (pbuh) that they would believe in him if he asked Allah to let them see Him in public.

Thunder shook the place. They were dazed and might have been destroyed but for Allah's mercy on the intercession of Moses (pbuh), who prayed that if it had been Allah's will, He could have, long before, destroyed both them and him. He asked Allah whether He would destroy them for the deeds of the foolish ones among them.

Moses (pbuh) pleaded for mercy for those who erred, for they did this from weakness and not from disobedience.

In his prayer, he addressed his Lord as Protector, and asked for His forgiveness and mercy. Moses also asked Allah to ordain for them that which was good to them, in this life and in the Hereafter (7:155–156).

To deface the wealth features of Pharaoh and his chiefs

To harden their hearts so that they would not believe until they see the grievous Chastisement

Allah sent Moses (pbuh) and his brother Aaron with His Signs to Pharaoh and his chiefs, who were wicked and arrogant. When Allah's Truth was shown to them, they said it was indeed evident sorcery, magic performed with the aid of evil spirits.

Moses (pbuh) denounced what they said.

They told him no matter what it was, they would not believe in him, adding that he had come to them to turn them away from the ways they found their fathers following, so that he and his brother might have greatness in the land.

Moreover, they attributed to Moses (pbuh) the very evil motives he had been sent to put down, namely, ambition and lust of power.

"Bring me every sorcerer well versed," Pharaoh ordered his chiefs.

When the sorcerers came, Moses (pbuh) said to them, "Throw you what you wish to throw!"

They threw their rods and in the eyes of the people, by a trick of sorcery, these rods became snakes. This struck terror into the crowd.

"Throw your rod," Allah ordered Moses (pbuh).

He did, and it swallowed all that which the sorcerers had faked. The illusion was broken and the falsehood was all shown up.

Pharaoh's sorcerers believed in Moses (pbuh). So did Pharaoh's wife.

Of Moses' people, only some believed in him. They feared Pharaoh and his chiefs, lest they should persecute them, for certainly Pharaoh was mighty on the earth and one who transgressed all bounds.

Moses (pbuh) said on behalf of himself and his brother Aaron, "Our Lord! You have indeed bestowed on Pharaoh and his Chiefs splendour and wealth in this life of the present, and so, Our Lord, they mislead men from Your Path. Deface, Our Lord, the features of their wealth, and send hardness to their hearts, so they will not believe until they see the grievous Chastisement (10:88)."

Allah accepted Moses and Aaron's prayer, and ordered them to stand out straight for Truth.

Allah took the people of Moses (pbuh) across the sea. Pharaoh and his army followed them in insolence and spite.

At length, when overwhelmed with the flood, Pharaoh said that he believed that there was no god except Allah, Whom

Moses and his followers believed in.

This was death-bed repentance, forced by the terror of drowning. So it was not accepted in its entirety. Only the body was saved from the sea and, presumably, it was embalmed and the mummy was given due rites of the dead.

Prophet David (pbuh)

To forgive him for having overlooked Allah's grace to him

David (pbuh) was a pious man, and he had a well-guarded private chamber for prayer and praise. He used to retire to it for devotion at stated times.

One day two men climbed over the wall of David's chamber and entered to him. He was terrified by this sudden appearance of the two men before him.

One of them told him not to fear them, and explained that they were two disputants, one of whom had wronged the other, and he asked David to decide between them with truth, and not to treat them with injustice, but to guide them to the even path.

These disputants were brothers. The one more aggrieved said that his brother had a flock of ninety-nine sheep, while he himself had only one, and that his brother wanted him to give up his one sheep to him, adding that he talked to him like one meditating mischief against him. Then he asked David to tell him what to do.

David (pbuh) told him that his brother had undoubtedly wronged him in demanding his single sheep to be added to his flock of sheep. Then he spoke of how wrong it was for brothers or men in partnership to take advantage of each other, and how few were the men who were righteous.

Had David in his mind his own devotion and justice when he spoke to the man? That is, did he mean to make a show?

In fact there was something vague in this case. It was not clear why the unjust brother, who said nothing, should have come with the complainant, risking his life in climbing the wall. Moreover, the men disappeared as mysteriously as they had come.

David (pbuh) realized that the incident had been a trial or a test of his moral character. Great though he was as a king, and just though he was as a judge, the moment that he thought of these things, that is, being a great king and a just judge, his merit vanished. In himself he was as other men. It was Allah's grace that gave him wisdom and justice, and he should have been humble in the sight of Allah.

Judged by ordinary standards, David's fault here was his hastiness in judging before hearing the case from the other party. Judged by the higher standard of those nearest to Allah, the thought of self-pride and self-righteousness had to be washed off from him by his own act of self-realisation and repentance.

So he asked forgiveness of his Lord. He fell down, bowing in prostration, and turned to Allah in repentance (38:24).

Allah forgave him and told him that He had bestowed on him wisdom, justice and all the other great gifts as a trust. These gifts were not to be a matter of self-glory.

Prophet Solomon (pbuh)

To forgive him and grant him a kingdom never to be granted to anyone after him

One afternoon Solomon (pbuh) was watching his horses trot

before him. They were swift and of the highest breeding. As he was reviewing his fine horses, time was due for his evening devotion, but he did not notice that until after sunset. He was overwhelmed by his horses.

He did his worship and ordered the horses to be brought back. "Then he began to pass his hand over their legs and their necks", says *The Holy Qur'an*. One interpretation of this quoted sentence is that as Solomon (pbuh) was so engrossed in the inspection of his fine horses that he completely forgot to remember his afternoon worship, he slaughtered them for food to the poor. Another interpretation is that like all lovers of horses, he patted them on their necks and passed his hands over their fore-legs and was proud of having them.

Allah tested Solomon (pbuh) with a severe illness, and he realized how weak and powerless he was. So he turned to Allah with humility, and said, "O my Lord! Forgive me, and grant me a Kingdom which will not belong to another after me, for You are the Grantor of Bounties without measure (38:35)."

Allah forgave him and answered his wishes. He subjected the wind to Solomon's power, to flow gently to his order, to where ever he willed. Allah also brought Satan to Solomon's command.

Solomon (pbuh) enjoyed a place so close to Allah.

To make him grateful for the favours granted to him and to his parents, and to make him work the righteousness that will please Allah
To admit him to the ranks of Allah's righteous servants

Solomon (pbuh) was a king of power and authority. He had influence among peoples outside his kingdom. He had knowledge of birds, beasts, and plants. He had something of all kinds of desirable gifts, and he referred them all to Allah with true gratitude.

Solomon (pbuh) and his army of men, birds, and jinns came to a valley of ants. A jinn was a spirit that could appear in human or animal form and do good or harm to people.

One of the ants said, "O you ants, get into your habitations, lest Solomon and his hosts crush you under foot without knowing it."

Solomon (pbuh) heard the ant and smiled, amused at her speech, and he said, "O my Lord! So order me that I may be grateful for Your favours, which You have bestowed on me and on my parents, and that I may work the righteousness that will please You, and admit me by Your Grace, to the ranks of Your righteous servants (27:19)."

Prophet Jonah (pbuh)

To accept his repentance

Jonah's mission (pbuh) was to Nineveh, a glorious city of the past, about two hundred and thirty miles north of Baghdad.

There came a time when Nineveh became a city of sin. Allah sent Jonah (pbuh) to warn its inhabitants. He warned them time and again, but they rejected his warnings.

Jonah (pbuh) condemned his people wrathfully and, exasperated, he ran away from Nineveh, went off to the shore, and took a ship.

The ship met foul weather and it was fully laden. The sailors, compelled by their superstition that a fugitive slave would cause such ill-luck, wanted to find out who was responsible for the ill-luck. The lot fell on Jonah (pbuh), and he was cast off.

A whale swallowed him, but he did not lose his life.

The Tigris River contained some fishes of extraordinary size, and the whale that swallowed Jonah (pbuh) was a fish of this size.

It was clear now to him that he had wronged himself. He should have stuck to the mission Allah had assigned to him.

He repented and glorified Allah. In the depth of darkness, he cried, "There is no god but You. Glory be to You. I was indeed wrong (21:87)!"

Jonah (pbuh) repented, and Allah accepted his repentance. Had he not done so, he could have died and stayed in the body of that fish until the Day of Resurrection, when all the dead would be raised up.

Allah cast him forth on the shore in a state of sickness, and caused a spreading plant of the gourd kind to grow over him. This plant gave him shade and sustenance.

Jonah was sent back to Nineveh, with a different state of mind. Its inhabitants listened to him and accepted Allah's Message.

Prophet Zakariya (pbuh)

To give him an heir

Zakariya (pbuh) raised the following prayer: "O my Lord! Infirm indeed are my bones, and the hair of my head does glisten with grey. But never am I unblest, O my Lord, in my prayer to You! Now I fear what my relatives and colleagues will do after me, as my wife is barren. So give me an heir as from Yourself, one that will truly inherit me, and inherit the posterity of Jacob; and make him, O my Lord! One with whom You are well-pleased (19:4–7)!"

Zakariya (pbuh) was a descendant of Prophet Jacob (pbuh).

His prayer was answered. "O Zakariya! We give you good news of a son. His name shall be Yahya. On none by that name have We conferred distinction before."

Bewildered, Zakariya (pbuh) said, "O my Lord! How shall I have a son, when my wife is barren and I have grown quite decrepit from old age? Can it really be so? Can I really have a son in my old age?"

The angel-messenger said, "Your Lord says that that is easy for Him. He did indeed create you before, when you had been nothing!'"

Zakariya (pbuh) said, "O my Lord! Give me a Sign." The answer was the following: "Your Sign shall be that you shall speak to no man for three nights, although you are not dumb."

Zakariya (pbuh) came out to his people from his chamber. He told them by signs to celebrate Allah's praises in the morning and in the evening.

Time passed and the son was born and grown up. Allah's command to him was to keep fast with all his might, his hold of Allah's revelation. Allah gave him wisdom even as a youth, and gave him purity and pity for all creatures.

Yahya was devout and kind to his parents. He was not overbearing or rebellious.

Prophet Jesus Christ (pbuh)

To send from heaven to him and to his people a table set with choice food, and to provide for their sustenance

Allah strengthened Prophet Jesus Christ (pbuh) with the Holy Spirit, so that he did speak to the people in childhood and in old age, and He taught him the Torah and the Gospel.

By Allah's leave, Jesus (pbuh) made out of clay, as it were, the figure of a bird, and he breathed into it, and it became a bird. Also by Allah's leave, he healed those born blind, and the lepers. And he brought forth the dead by Allah's leave, too.

Jesus Christ (pbuh) showed the Children of Israel, that is, the descendants of Prophet Jacob (pbuh), who is called Israel in *The Holy Qur'an* for his obedience, the Clear Signs by Allah's leave, so that they would believe him as Allah's Messenger to them. The unbelievers among them said that that was nothing but evident magic. Allah did restrain them from violence to him.

Allah inspired the Disciples of Jesus Christ (pbuh) to have faith in His Messenger. They said that they had faith, and asked Jesus to bear witness that they bow to Allah in obedience.

They asked Jesus (pbuh) if his Lord could send down to them a Table set with viands from Heaven. He told them to fear Allah, if they had faith. They said that they only wished to eat thereof and satisfy their hearts, and to know that he had indeed told them the truth about himself, and that they themselves might be witnesses to the miracle.

Jesus Christ (pbuh) said, "O Allah our Lord! Send us from heaven a table set with viands, that there may be for us – for the first and the last of us – a solemn festival and a Sign from You; and provide for our sustenance, for You are the best Sustainer of our needs (5:114)."

Allah said, "I will send it down unto you. But if any of you after that resists faith, I will punish him with a chastisement such as I have not inflicted on anyone among all the peoples."

Prophet Muhammad (pbuh)

To assist him in the battle of Badr

Prophet Muhammad (pbuh) prayed Allah for assistance in the battle of Badr, and Allah answered his prayer, saying, "Remember you implored the assistance of your Lord, and He answered you: 'I will assist you with a thousand of the angels, ranks on ranks' (8:9)."

Allah sent angels to fight on Muhammad's side (pbuh) against the unbelievers who fought him and his followers. Allah told the angels that He would instill terror into their enemies' hearts. He ordered them to smite their fingertips off them, so that their hands would be put out of action, and become unable to wield their sword or lance, and get easily defeated.

Before the battle, Allah made Muhammad (pbuh) and his followers feel drowsy, and calmed them. And He caused rain to descend on them to clean them and remove from them the stain of Satan, so as to strengthen their hearts.

Muhammad (pbuh) and his companions stood firm in the battlefield. The spirit of calm confidence on their part won against the blustering violence of their enemy.

CHAPTER V

Prayers of Believers

Believers asked Allah to guide them to the straight way; not to condemn them if they forgot or fell into error; not to lay on them a burden like that which He laid on those before them, nor a burden greater than they were able to bear; to blot out their sins; to grant them His forgiveness; to have mercy on them; and to help them overcome the unbelievers.

The foremost in doing good among believers prayed that praise be to Allah.

The migrants from Makkah and the inhabitants of Al Madinah prayed Allah to forgive them and those who came before them into the Faith, and not to leave in their hearts resentment or any sense of injury against them.

The firm and steadfast prayed Allah to forgive them their sins, and to help them against resistants of Faith.

The fighters in the battle of Uhud prayed to be firm in their belief that Allah alone was their best Guardian.

The Muslims oppressed in Makkah prayed Allah to rescue them from oppressors, and to raise for them a protector.

The servants of Allah prayed Him to forgive them their sins, and to save them from the agony of the Fire.

Paradise dwellers prayed that glory and praise be to Allah.

The knowledgeable prayed Allah not to let their hearts deviate from the right way, to grant them mercy, to let glory be to Allah, to save them from the chastisement of the Fire, to forgive them their sins, to wipe out iniquities, to place them in the company of the righteous, to give them what He promised through His Messengers, and to save them from shame on the Day of Judgment.

The humane prayed Allah to turn away from them the fury of Hell, to grant them righteous wives and children, to give them the favour to lead the righteous.

Solicitors of the good in both this world and the Hereafter prayed Allah to give them this good, and to save them from the torment of Hell.

The disciples of Jesus Christ (pbuh) and the Ethiopian Christians prayed Allah to write them down among those who bear witness.

Pharaoh's sorcerers asked Allah, after they repented, to pour patience and constancy out on them, and take their souls unto Him as Muslims who bow to His Will.

The righteous among Moses' people (pbuh) asked Allah not to make them a trial for oppressors, and to deliver them from those who rejected Allah.

Talut's men asked Allah to let constancy pour on them and make their steps firm, and to help them against those who reject Faith.

The Companions of the Cave asked Allah to bestow on them mercy from Him, and to settle their affairs for them in the right way.

The wife of Imran asked Allah to accept her dedication of the child she bore for Allah's special service.

The faithful son at forty asked Allah to let him be grateful for Allah's favours to himself and to his parents, and to grant him graciousness in his offspring.

The better one of two contestants asked Allah to give him something better than the other man's garden, and to send thunderbolts to this garden or to cause its water to be lost underground.

A believer among the people of Pharaoh asked Allah to accept his delegation of his affair to Him.

Finally, the wife of Pharaoh asked Allah to build for her a mansion in Paradise, and to save her from Pharaoh and all those who did wrong.

Believers in General

To show them the straight way

Believers seek Allah for guidance. They start their daily canonical prostrations in prayer with the name of Allah and His attribute of Mercy. Then they praise Him as the Lord who cares for all His creatures, and as the Master of the Day of Judgment.

They say emphatically, "You do we worship, and Your aid we seek." By the plural "we", they associate themselves with all seekers of Allah, so as to strengthen each other in a fellowship of faith. Then they say, "Show us the straight way (1:6)."

They ask Allah to help them find the way and stay in it. Without His help, they may not find the way or stay in it after they find it. They ask Him for the way of the people who live in the light of His Grace, and not the way of those who deliberately break Allah's law and live in the darkness of wrath, and not the way of those who stray out of carelessness.

This prayer sums up the faith and aspiration of those who offer themselves to Allah and seek His light.

Not to condemn them if they forget or fall into error
Not to lay on them a burden like that which He did lay on those before them
Not to lay on them a burden greater than they have strength to bear
To blot out their sins
To grant them forgiveness
To have mercy on them
To grant them victory over the unbelievers

Believers know that it is not for them to make any distinction between one and another of Allah's Messengers. They must honour them all equally.

Their faith is sincere. When their conduct is true to it, they realize how far from perfection they are. So they need Allah for the forgiveness of their shortcomings.

They know that Allah imposes no burden on them that they cannot bear. However, they still need Him to help them fulfill their duties. They know also that they need to exert themselves and try their best to be better off than those before them.

They say, "Our Lord! Condemn us not if we forget or fall into error. Our Lord! Lay not on us a burden like that which You did lay on those before us. Our Lord! Lay not on us a burden greater than we have strength to bear. Blot out our sins. And grant us forgiveness. Have mercy on us. You are our Protector. Grant us victory over the unbelievers (2:286)."

The Foremost in Doing Good

Praise be to Allah for having settled us in Paradise and for having removed from us all sorrow

The Holy Qur'an is the last Book revealed, and the followers of Prophet Muhammad (pbuh) are ordered to spread it among all mankind.

Believers are not all true to their charge, however. Some have problems in their conduct or intentions. Others do not, but they have much to learn yet. A third category may not be perfect, but both their intentions and their conduct are sound. They form an example to other men because they are 'foremost' in every good deed, not by merits of their own, but by the Grace of Allah.

The foremost will reach the highest achievement. They will enter the Gardens of Eternity. They will be adorned there with bracelets of gold and pearls, and their garments will be of silk.

They will say, "Praise be to Allah, Who has removed from us all sorrow, for our Lord is indeed oft-forgiving, ready to appreciate service. He has settled us in a Home that will last forever, where there won't be any toil (35:34–35)."

In Paradise all the hopes of those who are foremost in every good deed will be fulfilled.

The prayer for praise to be to Allah is also raised by those who are led to the Garden in groups. When these Believers arrive there, the angels keeping its gates will open them, and greet these groups with the salutation of peace, congratulate them, and welcome them in.

They will say, "Praise be to Allah, Who has truly fulfilled His promise to us, and has given us this land in heritage. We can dwell in the Garden as we will (39:74)!"

Migrants from Makkah and the Inhabitants of Al Madinah

To forgive them together with those who came before them into the Faith

Prophet Muhammad (pbuh) migrated with some of his followers from Makkah to Al Madinah. The inhabitants of Al Madinah had accepted Islam, and their goodwill and generous hospitality made the Prophet's migration possible.

His followers from Makkah, expelled from their homes and their property, were indeed a good example of the truthful. So were the people of Al Madinah. They accepted Islam when it was persecuted in Makkah, invited the holy Prophet to their town and became his followers, and they showed their affection to the Prophet's followers from Makkah.

The most remarkable ties of full brotherhood in Islam were established between individual members of the one group and the other. Al Madinah members regularly gave and the refugees regularly received. Even the poor vied with the rich in their spirit of self-sacrifice.

These Believers say, "Our Lord! Forgive us, and our brethren who came before us into the Faith and leave not, in our hearts, rancor or sense of injury against those who have believed. Our Lord! You are indeed Full of Kindness, Most Merciful (59:10)."

They prayed that their hearts may be purified of any desire or tendency to depreciate the work or virtues of other Muslims, or to feel any jealousy on account of their successes or good fortune.

The Firm and Steadfast

To forgive them their sins and any wrong they may have done, and to establish their feet firmly and help them against resistants of Faith

Prophet Muhammad (pbuh) was no more than a Messenger, a mortal like any human being. Many were the Messengers who passed away before him. If he died or were slain, would a Muslim then turn back on his heels? If he did, he would not do the least harm to Allah.

Nobody can die except by Allah's leave, and the term of life is fixed by Him. If anyone deserves a reward in this life or in the Hereafter, Allah shall give it to him. Allah rewards those who serve Him with gratitude.

Prophets together with their followers fought for the victory of Allah's way. They never lost heart if they met with disaster, nor did they weaken in will. Allah loves those who are firm and steadfast.

These Believers, the firm and steadfast, said, "Our Lord! Forgive us our sins and anything we may have done that transgressed our duty. Establish our feet firmly in the face of trouble, and help us against those who resist faith (3:147)."

Allah gave them a reward in this world, and He will give them another in the Hereafter. Allah loves those who do good.

Fighters in the Battle of Uhud

To be firm in the belief that Allah alone was their best Guardian

A number of the Muslim fighters were wounded in the battle of Uhud, and there was confusion after the battle. Some of them rallied around Prophet Muhammad (pbuh), who was wounded, too. But they were all ready to fight again.

The Unbelievers' leader, Abu Sufyan, with his Makkan

followers withdrew, leaving a challenge with the Prophet to meet him and his army again next year at the fair of the Badr Sughra, a region south of Al Madinah. The challenge was accepted.

Some people tried to frighten the Muslims. They told them that a great army was gathering against them. They would better fear them. But they did not fear them. This warning increased their faith that Allah would grant them victory. They said, "For us Allah sufficeth, and He is the best Guardian (3:173)."

They came to the appointed place at the appointed time, but the enemy did not come. They returned, unharmed.

Muslims Oppressed in Makkah

To rescue them from oppressors
To raise for them from Him one who will protect and help

The Muslims in Makkah suffered from oppression. They were mocked, assaulted and beaten. Those within the power of the Unbelievers were put into chains and cast into prison. Others were boycotted, and shut out of trade and business. They could not even buy the food they needed, or perform their religious duties.

The oppression was redoubled for Makkan Muslims after the departure or Hijrat of Prophet Muhammad (pbuh) at the order of Allah from Makkah to Al Madinah. They raised the following prayer: "Our Lord! Rescue us from this town, whose people are oppressors; and raise for us from You one who will protect; and raise for us from You one who will help (4:75)!"

Their prayer was answered when Prophet Muhammad (pbuh) brought freedom and peace to Makkah.

Servants of Allah

To forgive them their sins
To save them from the the agony of the Fire

The righteous are the true servants of Allah. They have faith, humility, hope, patience, steadfastness, and self-restraint.

The best of their goals to them is to be with Allah. Women and children, gold and silver, horses, cattle, and well-tilled land are the possessions of this world's life. But far better than those for the righteous are Gardens in nearness to their Lord, with rivers flowing beneath. Therein they look forward to having their eternal home, with their purified spouses. The good pleasure of Allah is far better in their eyes than things coveted in this life.

They show patience, they are true in word and deed, they worship devoutly, they are ready to spend in charity, and they pray for forgiveness in the early hours of the morning.

They say, "Our Lord! We have indeed believed. Forgive us, then, our sins, and save us from the agony of the Fire (3:16)."

Paradise Dwellers

Glory and praise be to Allah

Allah guides those who believe and work righteousness to their faith, which will in turn lead them to paradise.

In paradise, joy will fill their hearts. They will sing with ecstasy. Their greetings will be of peace and harmony. They will pray that glory and praise be to Allah, the cherisher and sustainer of all creatures (10:10).

The Knowledgeable

Not to let their hearts deviate from the right way
To grant them mercy

Believers are firmly grounded in their knowledge of Islam. They read *The Holy Qur'an*, and believe it is entirely from Allah.

They have faith. They wish to hold fast in their hearts the glimpses of truth they get.

They are sure of their eventual return to Allah. They believe that Allah is the one who will gather mankind together on a day about which there is no doubt.

They raise the following prayer: "O Lord! Let not our hearts deviate now after You have guided us, but grant us mercy from You. For You are the Grantor of bounties without measure (3:8)." They ask Allah to help them not lose the right way, and to give them His mercy.

Glory be to Allah
To save them from the chastisement of the Fire
To forgive them their sins
To wipe out their iniquities
To be in the company of the righteous
To give them what He promised through His Messengers
To save them from shame on the Day of Judgment

There are indeed signs for men of understanding in the creation of the heavens and the earth, and the alteration of night and day. These signs are brief symbols of the glorious majesty of Allah and His goodness to man.

These men remember Allah in all their circumstances, and

contemplate the wonders of creation in the heavens and the earth, saying that Allah has created all this not for nothing.

They pray that Glory be to Him, and they ask Him to save them from the chastisement of the Fire. They know that any whom He admits to the Fire, truly He covers with shame, and they know that wrong-doers will never find any helpers.

They say to Allah that they have heard the call of one inviting them to believe in the Lord, and that they have believed.

They say, "Our Lord! Forgive us our sins, blot out from us our iniquities, and take our souls to Yourself in the company of the righteous. Our Lord! Grant us what You did promise unto us through Your Messengers, and save us from shame on the Day of Judgment, for You never break Your promise (3:191–194)."

Their Lord accepts their prayer. He will never allow anyone of them, male or female, to suffer. In Paradise, He will reward them with lofty mansions with rivers flowing beneath them.

The Humane

To turn away from them the fury of Hell
     To grant them righteous wives and children
     To give them the favour to lead the righteous

These believers are modest. When the morally ignorant address them aggressively, they respond peacefully.

They spend the night in adoration of their Lord, prostrate and standing. Their humble prayer brings them nearer to Him. They say, "Our Lord! Avert from us the Wrath of Hell, for its Wrath is indeed a grievous affliction – evil indeed it is as an abode, and as a place to rest in (25:65–66)."

They are wise in their expenditure. They limit it to what is necessary. They are not extravagant, nor niggardly. They hold a just balance between these two extremes.

They do not invoke with Allah any other god.

They do not commit fornication. They know that anyone who does this, will meet punishment not in this life only, but will be doubly punished on the Day of Judgment, unless he repents.

When asked, they do not give false evidence, nor do they assist at anything which implies fraud. In addition, if any one of them finds himself in the midst of futilities such as vain talk, unedifying jokes, or useless show, he withdraws from it calmly, in an honourable, dignified way.

When the Signs of their Lord are presented to these believers, they do not droop down at them, or behave as if they were deaf or blind.

They raise the following prayer: "Our Lord! Grant unto us wives and offspring who will be the comfort of our eyes, and give us the grace to lead the righteous (25:74)."

For their patient constancy, they will be rewarded with the highest place in heaven, where they will be met with salutation and peace.

Solicitors of the Good in This World and the Hereafter

To give them the good in both this world and the Hereafter, and to save them from the torment of Hell

There are people who pray for the bounties in this life only, and there are people who pray for the bounties in both this life and the Hereafter. Believers do not renounce this world, nor are they engrossed in it as to forget the Hereafter.

They say, "Our Lord! Give us good in this world and good

in the Hereafter. And save us from the torment of the Fire! (2:201).”

These people will be allotted what they have earned. Both their good and bad deeds go before them to the judgment seat of Allah. These deeds are witnesses for or against them, and their good or bad influence begins to operate before they know it.

The Disciples of Jesus Christ (pbuh)

To write them down among those who bear witness

The angels told Mary that Allah would give her glad tidings of a Word from Him. His name would be Christ Jesus, the son of Mary, held in honour in this world and the Hereafter. The angels added that he would speak to the people in childhood and in maturity, and that he would be in the company of the righteous.

Mary asked how she should have a son when no man had touched her, and she was answered that Allah creates what He wills; when He has decreed a matter, He only says to it, ‘Be,’ and it is!

The angels continued that Allah would teach her son the Torah and the Gospel, and appoint him a Messenger to the Children of Israel, with the following message:

“I have come to you, with a Sign from your Lord, in that I make for you out of clay, as it were, the figure of a bird, and breathe into it, and it becomes a bird by Allah’s leave; and I heal those born blind, and the lepers, and I declare to you what you eat, and what you store in your houses. Surely therein is a Sign for you if you do believe.

“I have come to attest the Torah which was before me, and to make lawful to you part of what was before forbidden to you.

I have come to you with a Sign from your Lord. So fear Allah and obey me.

"It is Allah who is my Lord and your Lord; then do worship Him. This is a Way that is straight."

When Jesus found that they did not believe him, he said, "Who will be my helpers in the work of Allah?"

The Disciples said, "We are Allah's helpers. We believe in Allah, and do you bear witness of our submission to Him."

They added, "Our Lord! We believe in what You have revealed, and we follow the Messenger; then write us down among those who bear witness (3:53)."

The Ethiopian Christians

To write them down among the witnesses

The Christians of Ethiopia were friendly to the Muslim refugees who came to their country during the persecution of Believers in Makkah. They appreciated Muslim virtues. Among them were men devoted to learning, and they were not arrogant.

When these Christians of Ethiopia listened to *The Holy Qur'an,* the revelation received by the refugees' Messenger, they recognized the truth, and their eyes were tearful.

They prayed, "Our Lord! We believe. Write us down among the witnesses. What cause can we have not to believe in Allah and the truth which has come to us, seeing that we long for our Lord to admit us to the company of the righteous (5:83–84)?"

Allah accepted their prayer. He rewarded them with an eternal home in Heaven, with rivers flowing underneath them. Such is the recompense of those who do good.

Pharaoh's Repentant Sorcerers

To pour out on them patience and constancy, and take their souls unto Him as Muslims who bow to His Will

Moses told Pharaoh that he was a Messenger from the Lord of the Worlds, and that he had come to him and to his people with a clear Sign, so that they would let the Children of Israel, that is, the descendants of Prophet Jacob (pbuh) whom Allah had called Israel for his obedience, depart along with him.

Pharaoh asked Moses to show his Sign.

Moses threw his rod, and it was a serpent, plain for all to see. Then he drew his hand from the folds of his garment, and it was white and shining as with divine light.

The Chiefs of the people of Pharaoh said that Moses was indeed a skilled sorcerer, with a plan to drive out the Egyptians from their own land. They advised Pharaoh to keep Moses and his brother in suspense for a while, and to send to the cities men to collect the most skilled sorcerers.

These magicians came to Pharaoh. They asked him for a reward if they won. He promised to give them not only that but also high positions in his Court.

They asked Moses whether he wished the first throw to be for himself or for them. Moses asked them to throw first.

They did, showing a great feat of magic. The beholders were bewitched and struck with terror.

Allah revealed to Moses to throw his rod, and watch. It swallowed up all the falsehoods which the sorcerers faked. The truth was thus confirmed, and all that Pharaoh's sorcerers did lost its effect.

At once Pharaoh's sorcerers recognized the Signs of Allah.

So they turned humble. They fell down prostrate in adoration. Their conscience was awakened, saying that they believed in the Lord of the Worlds, the Lord of Moses and Aaron.

Pharaoh threatened them with extreme punishment. He would crucify them all and cut off their hands and their feet on opposite sides. But they remained firm, and prayed to Allah for patience and constancy saying, "Our Lord! Pour out on us patience and constancy, and take our souls unto You as Believers who bow to Your Will (7:126)!"

The Righteous among Moses' People (pbuh)

Not to make them a trial for oppressors, and to deliver them from those who rejected Allah

The majority of Moses' people (pbuh) feared Pharaoh, lest he should persecute them, as he certainly was mighty on the earth, and one who transgressed all bounds.

Moses (pbuh) addressed his people dearly, saying that if they did really believe in Allah and submitted their will to Him, then in Him they should put their trust.

Those who had faith in Allah's providence were only a few. They said in Allah did they put their trust, and raised the following prayer: "Our Lord, make us not a trial for those who practice oppression; and deliver us by Your Mercy from those who reject You (10:85–86)."

Allah inspired Moses (pbuh) and his brother Aaron to provide dwellings for their people in Egypt, to make their dwellings places of worship, to establish regular prayers, and to give glad tidings to those who believed.

Talut's Men

To let constancy pour on them and make their steps firm, and to help them against those who reject Faith

Long after Moses (pbuh) and Aaron, there came a time when the Children of Israel, that is, the descendants of Prophet Jacob (pbuh) asked their Prophet to appoint a king for them to fight under his command in the cause of Allah. Their Prophet asked them whether it was not possible if they were commanded to fight, that they would not fight. They told him how they could refuse to fight in the cause of Allah, being turned out of their homes and families.

But later when they were commanded to fight, they turned back, except a small band among them.

Their Prophet told them that Allah had appointed Talut as king over them. Talut was tall and handsome, but he belonged to a small tribe. They first rejected Talut, saying that they were better fitted than he was to exercise authority. Their Prophet told them that Allah had chosen Talut above them, and had gifted him abundantly with knowledge and bodily prowess.

He also told them that a Sign of Talut's authority was that there should come to them, carried by angels, a chest of acacia wood covered with gold, with an assurance therein of security from their Lord, and the relics left by the family of Moses (pbuh) and the family of Aaron.

Talut set forth with the armies.

He knew that a commander is hampered by a large force if it is not in perfect discipline and does not wholeheartedly believe in its Commander, and he knew as well that he must get rid of all the doubtful individuals under his command.

So he said, "Allah will test you at the stream; if any drinks of its water, he goes not with my army. A mere sip out of the hand is excused."

They drank of the stream water, except a few.

These crossed the river with Talut and, when they met the enemy face to face, they said, "This day we cannot cope with Goliath and his forces."

Among them there was a very small number who had perfect confidence in Allah and in the cause for which they were fighting. They said, "How often, by Allah's will, has a small force vanquished a big one? Allah is with those who steadfastly persevere."

They advanced to meet their enemy, praying, "Our Lord! Pour out constancy on us and make our steps firm. Help us against those who reject faith (2:250)."

By Allah's will, they conquered their enemy.

Companions of the Cave

To bestow on them mercy from Him, and to settle their affair for them in the right way

A number of youths left the town to escape persecution, and went to a cave in a mountain near by. They fell asleep, and remained so for some generations or centuries. Their story became very popular.

The unbelievers in Makkah were in the habit of asking Prophet Muhammad (pbuh) questions which they thought the Prophet would not be able to answer. In this way, they hoped to discredit him.

One of these questions was about the story of the Youths of

the Cave.

Allah told his Prophet the following story in a revelation: They were young men who believed in Allah, and by His grace and mercy, they knew that He was the Lord of the heavens and of the earth. They saw that their people were wrong in taking for worship another god.

By the will of Allah, the youths took their way to the mountain and in a cave there, they said, "Our Lord! Bestow on us mercy from Yourself, and dispose of our affair for us in the right way (18:10)!"

Their prayer was heard and Allah promised to help them against all odds.

Having faith and trust in Allah, they found safety and refuge in the Cave. They were protected from the persecution and violence of the heathen.

They were completely cut off from the outer world for a number of years. It was as if they had died, with their knowledge and ideas remaining at the point of time when they had entered the Cave.

Allah roused the young men from their unconsciousness, and asked them how long they had tarried. Some said they had stayed perhaps a day or part of a day. Others gave different answers, so at length they all said Allah alone knows best how long they had stayed there.

By Allah's will, they sent one of them to the town to buy food. The money they carried was coined in the reign of the monarch who ruled at the time when they came to the Cave. They requested their Companion to find out which was the best food and to bring some of it to them, and to behave with care and courtesy, and not to inform any one about them.

They thought the world had not changed, and that the fierce

persecution they knew was still raging. That's why they feared that if the town people knew about them, they would stone them or force them to give up their faith.

Allah made their case known to the people so that they might know that His promise was true. It was by His will that they sent one of them with the old money to the town to buy provisions.

His dress, appearance, speech and old money at once drew the attention of people to him. They learnt his story and realised that Allah, Who can protect His servants thus and raise them up from sleep after such a long time, and that there could be no doubt that He has the power to raise up men for the Resurrection, and that His promise of goodness and mercy to those who serve Him, is true.

The Sleepers could not judge about the duration of their stay in the Cave, so they wisely left the matter and attended to the urgent business of their lives. The townsfolk could not agree to the significance of the event, so they fell to discussing immaterial details.

The real significance of the event lies not in the number of men in the Cave, nor in the duration of the time they stayed there, but in its spiritual lesson as explained in *The Holy Qur'an*: People must believe, as the Companions of the Cave did, that Allah knows best.

The Wife of Imran

To accept her dedication of the child she bears for Allah's special service

The wife of Imran, Anne, was a member of a priestly family. She was a relative to Prophet Zakariya (pbuh) and a descendant of Aaron, the brother of Prophet Moses (pbuh).

The wife of Imran said, "O my Lord! I do dedicate unto You what is in my womb for Your special service. So accept this of me, for You hear and know all things (3:35)."

She had expected a male child, and intended to devote him to temple service. But when she delivered, it was a female. She was not disappointed, however, for she had Faith, and she knew that Allah's Plan was better than any wishes of hers.

She named her female child Mary, and she had a sense of pride in the girl. She commended her and her offspring to the protection of Allah.

Allah accepted the prayer of the wife of Imran, and Mary grew under His special protection.

The angels told Mary that Allah had purified her and chosen her above the women of all nations. They requested her to worship the Lord devoutly, to let herself prostrate, and bow down in prayer with those who bow down.

Allah assigned Prophet Zakariya (pbuh) to look after her.

Every time Zakariya entered Mary's chamber to see her, he found her supplied with sustenance. Surprised, he asked her where that sustenance came from. She told him from Allah, for He, she added, provides sustenance to whom He pleases without measure.

The Faithful Son at Forty

To be grateful for Allah's favours to him and his parents,and for Allah's favour that he may work righteousness such as Allah may approve

To be granted Allah's graciousness in his offspring

Allah has enjoined children to be kind to their parents. A child's mother in pain did she bear him, and in pain did she give birth to him.

When a child is forty years old, the age of full strength, he says, "O my Lord! Grant me that I may be grateful for Your favour which You have bestowed upon me, and upon both my parents, and that I may work righteousness such as You may approve; and be gracious to me in my issue. Truly have I turned to You and truly do I submit to You in Islam (46:15)."

Allah accepts from people like this man the best of their deeds.

The Better One of Two Contestants

To give him something better than his neighbour's garden, and to send on his neighbour's garden thunderbolts or to let its water run off and be lost underground

Allah provided a man with two gardens of grape-vines and surrounded them with date palms. In between the two, He placed a piece of land good for tillage.

Allah also caused a river to flow between the two gardens.

Each garden brought forth its produce, not failing in the least in doing so. Abundant was the yield this man had.

He said to his neighbour in the course of a mutual argument: "More wealth have I than you, and more honour and power in my following of men." He took his neighbour with him to impress him with his own importance. He said that he did not think his garden would ever perish, nor did he think the Day of Judgment would ever come. He wronged himself.

His neighbour asked him whether he denied Allah, Who created him out of dust, then out of a sperm-drop, then fashioned him into a man. As for his part, he said that Allah was his Lord, and none will he associate with his Lord. He suggested to his neighbor that he'd better enjoy Allah's gift with gratitude to Him as he went into his garden, rather than brag about his having more wealth and sons than himself.

Then he said, "It may be that my Lord will give me something better than your garden, and that he will send on your garden thunderbolts by way of reckoning from heaven, making it slippery sand! Or the water of your garden will run off underground so that you will never be able to find it (18:40–41)."

The arrogant's fruits were encompassed with ruin, and he remained twisting and turning his hands over what he had spent on his property, which had now tumbled to pieces to its very foundations, and he said, "Woe is me! Would I were thankful and never ascribed partners to my Lord and Cherisher!"

He had great income and satisfaction. His thoughts had been wholly occupied by his property. It would not have gone had he only looked to Allah.

A Believer among the People of Pharaoh

To accept his delegation of his affair to Allah

There was a believer among the people of Pharaoh, who had concealed his faith. He said, referring to Moses (pbuh), "Will you slay a man because he says his Lord is Allah?" He told them that if Moses (pbuh) was a liar, the sin of his lie would be on him. But if he was telling the truth, then the calamity Moses (pbuh) was warning them against, would fall on them.

He pointed out that Allah did not guide one who broke a sacred law, and added that he feared for them something like the disasters of the peoples of Noah and of others who did not believe Allah's Messengers.

He explained that Allah never wished injustice to His servants, and warned them that unless they gave up evil, a day would come to them when they would turn their backs and flee, and they would have no defender from Allah, Who would leave them to stray, with none to guide them.

He told them about the mission of Joseph (pbuh) to their ancestors, saying that Joseph (pbuh) was a ruler and saviour to them in times of famine. They profited by the material gains which came to them through him, but remained sceptical of his spiritual truths. He added that Allah lets go wrong those who transgress and live in doubt.

He urged them to follow him, adding that he would lead them to the right way, and continued earnestly, "O my People! This life of the present is nothing but temporary enjoyment. It is the Hereafter that is the Home that will last. He who works evil will not be requited but by the like thereof, and he who works a righteous deed and is a believer will enter the Garden of Bliss, where he will have abundance without measure."

He told them that they would soon remember what he said to them, and concluded, "My own affair I commit to Allah, for Allah ever watches over His Servants (40:44)."

Allah saved him from every evil plotted against him. The people of Pharaoh were tortured in this world and would be tortured in the Hereafter.

The Wife of Pharaoh

To build for her a mansion in Paradise, and to save her from Pharaoh and all those who do wrong

Allah warns men against the fire of Hell. It is not merely like the physical fire which burns wood and consumes it, but it will have for its fuel people who do wrong and stones. They must carefully guard their own conduct, and that of their families.

There is no injustice in this fire imposed on unbelievers. They get there what they deserve, the fruit of their own deeds.

Believers are not infallible. They sin.

Allah exhorts the believers among married couples to turn to Him with sincere repentance. This will help them to realise that the good and righteous can retain their integrity even though their mates are evil.

Allah sets forth, as an example to unbelievers, the wife of Noah, who was false to the standards of her husband, and the wife of Lut, the world around whom was wicked and she followed it rather than her righteous husband. They were respectively under two righteous husbands, but they betrayed them. They could not plead that they were the wives of pious husbands. So they had to enter Hell like any other wicked woman. Responsibility before Allah is personal.

Allah gives Mary the daughter of Imran as an example of those women who believed. Mary was one of the purest of women. She guarded her chastity. She was one of the devout servants.

Allah sets forth the wife of Pharaoh as another example of those who believed. Her husband was arrogant, wicked, and godless. For her to have preserved her Faith in his house all the time, was indeed a great spiritual triumph.

She said, "O my Lord! Build for me, in nearness to You, a mansion in the Garden, and save me from Pharaoh and his doings, and save me from those that do wrong (66:11)."

Men on the Partition between Heaven and Hell

Not to send them to the company of the wrong-doers

There will be a partition between Heaven and Hell, and on its heights there will be such men as are not decidedly on the side of merit or decidedly on the side of sin.

These men would know everyone by his marks. They will greet the people of Heaven by "Peace be upon you", and invite them to enter the Garden, where there will be no fear on them, nor will they grieve.

When they turn towards the people of Hell, they will say, "Our Lord! Send us not to the company of the wrong-doers (7:47)."

CHAPTER VI

Prayers of Unbelievers

People not believing in the Hereafter prayed for the bounties of the present world.

Their followers prayed for a double chastisement and a curse to misleaders.

A married couple prayed to be thankful to Allah if He gave them a child sound in body and mind.

Seamen prayed to be thankful to Allah if He saved them from a sea storm.

The merchants of Saba prayed Allah to extend the distances between their caravan journey stations for monopoly purposes.

Hell dwellers prayed for a second chance in this world.

The scornful prayed for the removal of chastisement from them.

Mockers of their prophets prayed for hastening to them their punishment.

Finally, the infidels in Makkah prayed for a shower of stones on themselves.

People Unbelieving in the Hereafter

To give them the bounties in this life

Some people pray Allah for the good in both this life and that after death, and for safety from the torment of the Fire. Their attitude is neither to renounce this world nor to be so engrossed in it as to forget the Hereafter.

Other people do not believe there is a life after death. As a result, they would lose the higher things of the Hereafter. They say, "Our Lord! Give us the bounties in this world (2:200)!"

An extreme example of this type of people is that one whose speech about this life may be dazzling. He has a smooth tongue, and he indulges in plausible talk with many oaths. He calls Allah to witness about what is in his heart, while he is the most contentious of Allah's enemies.

Followers of the Unbelievers

To give misleaders double chastisement and a very great curse

Allah has condemned the Unbelievers and promised an everlasting, blazing fire for them. There they will find no protector or helper.

On the day of retribution they will be humiliated, and they will wish that they had followed right guidance when they had the chance.

They will then fall to accusing their leaders who misled them. They will say: "Our Lord! We obeyed our chiefs and our great ones, and they misled us as to the right path. Our Lord! Give them double chastisement and curse them with a very great curse (33:67–68)!"

They ask for double penalty to their leaders, blaming them for having been themselves misled, and for having misled others. They overlook their personal responsibility. It is the nature of evil to shift the blame on to others. But none can escape punishment for his own wrong-doings.

To give a double chastisement to whoever was responsible for their being in Hell

A troop of misleaders rushes into Hell. Those who were misled by them cry, "Nay, you too! No welcome for you! It is you who have brought this upon us!"

They raise the following prayer, asking for double punishment to them: "Our Lord! Whoever brought this upon us, add to him a double chastisement in the Fire (38:61)!"

The Unbelievers in Hell wonder why they do not see men whom they ridiculed as fools because they refused to join in with them in their plots. These were good men and they were not to be seen in Hell. Here the ridicule is reversed, now it is against the evil ones.

Parents Breaking Their Oath to Allah

To be grateful to Allah if He granted them a goodly child

A married woman bears a light burden and carries it about unnoticed. Then she grows heavy. When the child is yet unborn, and it stirs within the body of the expectant mother, she and her husband are both filled with much hope as well as much unknown risk to the mother herself.

In their anxiety, they both turn to Allah, saying, "If You give us a goodly child, we vow we shall ever be grateful (7:189)." They ask for a child who is sound in body and soul, and of good disposition.

When the child is born, the parents forget that it is a precious gift of Allah. Instead, their gradual familiarity with the child, makes them take it as a matter of course. They ascribe to others a share in the gift they have received.

Seamen Breaking Their Oath to Allah

To be grateful to Allah if He delivers them from a sea storm

People travel through land and sea by the will of Allah. In general, they turn their thoughts in adversity to Allah. As soon as the trouble is past, they forget Him.

Seamen sail on board a ship with a favourable wind, and that pleases them. Then comes a stormy wind, and the waves come to them from all sides, and they think that they are being overwhelmed.

They pray to Allah, saying, "If You do deliver us from this, we shall truly show our gratitude (10:22)!"

When He delivers them, however, they do not show their gratitude.

Allah says, "O mankind! Your insolence is against your own souls."

The Merchants of Saba

To place longer distances between their caravan stations

Saba was the name of a territory in Yemen. It was a rich, fertile country. The dam of Maarib made it very prosperous. Its roads were skirted by gardens on both sides. It produced fruit, spices, and frankincense.

Its well-doing was a sign from Allah to its people.

There was a great highway between Saba and the countries to the north. This highway was much frequented. It connected between the great and flourishing kingdoms of the Euphrates and Tigris valleys on the one hand, and Egypt on the other; and between the great Roman Empire around the Mediterranean.

To the south, through the Yemen Coast, the road connected, by sea transport with India, Malaya, and China.

Travel on these roads was secure, by night and by day. The cities on it were convenient stages of the journey, for merchants to trade their supplies.

The merchants of Saba wanted to get more profit from their supplies by concentrating them on a few stations, which they could monopolize.

They said, "Our Lord! Place longer distances between our journey-stations (34:19)."

Keeping profit entirely to oneself is a wrong-doing.

Allah sent a mighty flood against them, and the dam burst. The flourishing gardens were turned into waste. The sweet fruit trees gave place to wild plants with bitter fruit.

The grasping nature of the people of Saba, and their departure from the highest standards of righteousness, ruined the big trade and brought about the decline of Saba.

Those Praying for a Return to This World

Hell Dwellers

To bring them out of Hell

The dead will be raised up for judgment. They will each stand alone. The old relationships of the world will then be dissolved, and no one will ask after another.

Good and evil deeds will be weighed against each other. Those whose balance of good deeds is heavy will be in Heaven, but if it is light, they will be in Hell.

The Fire will burn their faces.

They will be asked whether Allah's Signs were not rehearsed to them, and whether these Signs were treated by them as falsehoods. They will admit that their misfortune overwhelmed them, and that they went astray.

They will be reminded of the ridicule with which they treated believers and of their laughing at them.

They will say, "Our Lord! Bring us out of this. If ever shall we return to evil, then shall we be wrong-doers indeed (23:107)!"

They will beg their Lord to bring them out of Hell in order that they may work righteousness in the things they neglected, adding that if ever they return to evil, then will they be wrong-doers indeed.

But it will be too late to ask for another chance. The time for repentance will then have passed. Their prayer will be treated merely as an empty word of excuse. They had plenty of chances for repentance in their life, but they rejected them.

They will be ordered not to speak to Allah.

The Guilty of Denying Resurrection

To send them back to the world to work righteousness

Everything is in Allah's power. He could have created a world in which there was no choice for man. But this was not His Will and Plan. Man has a certain amount of choice and free-will. That being so, Allah has provided Signs and means of instruction for him, in order that his will may be straight and pure.

Allah created man in proper proportions, and gave him the faculties of hearing, sight, and understanding, adapting him for the functions he has to perform.

Yet little thanks does man give.

He denies that there can be a future life. He asks how he will indeed be renewed in a new creation when he is laid, hidden and lost, in the earth.

He denies the meeting with his Lord.

Allah says this meeting will happen. He describes the guilty ones when they will meet with Him. They will bend low their heads before their Lord, saying, "Our Lord! We have seen and we have heard. Now then send us back to the world. We will work righteousness, for we do indeed now believe (32:12)."

Their prayer will be rejected.

The Ungrateful

To bring them out of Hell

Those who disobey Allah will be in Hell, where they will have pain, suffering, anguish, and humiliation.

They will cry aloud for assistance, "Our Lord! Bring us out. We shall work righteousness, not the deeds we used to do (35:37)." Their asking for another chance, however, after having deliberately rejected all chances, will be futile.

They had a long enough respite for repentance and amendment. Allah sent them a Messenger who taught them right from wrong, and warned them against doing wrong. They did not learn from him.

There will be no helper for the wrong-doers.

The Scornful

To remove the punishment from them

There is no god other than Allah. It is He Who gives life and death. He is the Lord and Cherisher to all people and their ancestors.

The Quraish, Prophet Muhammad's tribe (pbuh), received Allah's Message in the earlier stages of the preaching of Islam, with amusement. They played about with this Message, and expressed doubts about it. The Preacher, Muhammad (pbuh), who was one of them, was most earnest about it, with all his heart and soul in it. And he loved his people and wished to save them from their wickedness and folly.

How will the teaching of spiritual Truth make way among such unreasonable people? The Quraish had before them a Prophet whose purity of life was openly known to them. They themselves had described him worthy of all trust, and his preaching was clear and eloquent. Yet they turned away from him. They called him a madman, and claimed that his Message was not inspired by Allah, but written by some hidden hand!

Allah ordered His Prophet (pbuh) to watch for some calamity that was to happen soon afterwards.

A severe famine hit Makkah, in which men were so pinched with hunger that they saw mist before their eyes when they looked at the sky. The Makkans, who were pagans, attributed the famine to the curse of the Prophet (pbuh). Abu Sufyan, their chief, approached the holy Prophet (pbuh) to intercede and pray for the removal of the famine.

The famine enveloped the people, and they raised the

following prayer, "Our Lord! Remove the chastisement from us, for we do really believe (44:12)!"

Allah will indeed remove the chastisement for a while. He gives every chance to His creatures. He allows His Grace to work, again and again. Some are reclaimed, and some remain obdurate. Allah will give these the punishment they deserve.

Mockers of Their Prophets

To hasten to them their sentence

Those who did not believe in the Hereafter said ironically, "Our Lord! Hasten to us our sentence even before the Day of Account (38:16)!"

Allah ordered His prophets who were mocked to have patience at what the unbelievers said, and to remember men who had to exercise infinite patience when mocked by their contemporaries.

For example, when David (pbuh) was mocked, he always turned to Allah. He was a shepherd, and his brother chid him for deserting his sheep. When he came forward to fight Goliath, the giant mocked him. But his faith had made him more than a match for his enemy. He picked up pebbles from the stream, and used his sling to such effect that he knocked Goliath down, and slew him with his own sword. His faith was pure and it brought him Allah's reward.

The Infidels in Makkah

To rain down on them a shower of stones from the sky, or send them a grievous chastisement

The infidels in Makkah said, "O Allah! If this is indeed the Truth from You, rain down on us a shower of stones from the sky, or send us a grievous chastisement (8:32)."

This was a challenge thrown out by them not seriously but as a taunt. They did not believe that what they asked would really happen because they did not believe in Allah.

Allah did not answer their request for a number of reasons. He punishes in His own good time, not according to the foolish words of unbelievers. Another reason was that Prophet Muhammad (pbuh), who was the Mercy of the Worlds, was with them. His presence among them conferred a certain amount of immunity to them. A third reason was that there were also other Muslims among them, men who asked for forgiveness.

9 781804 394236